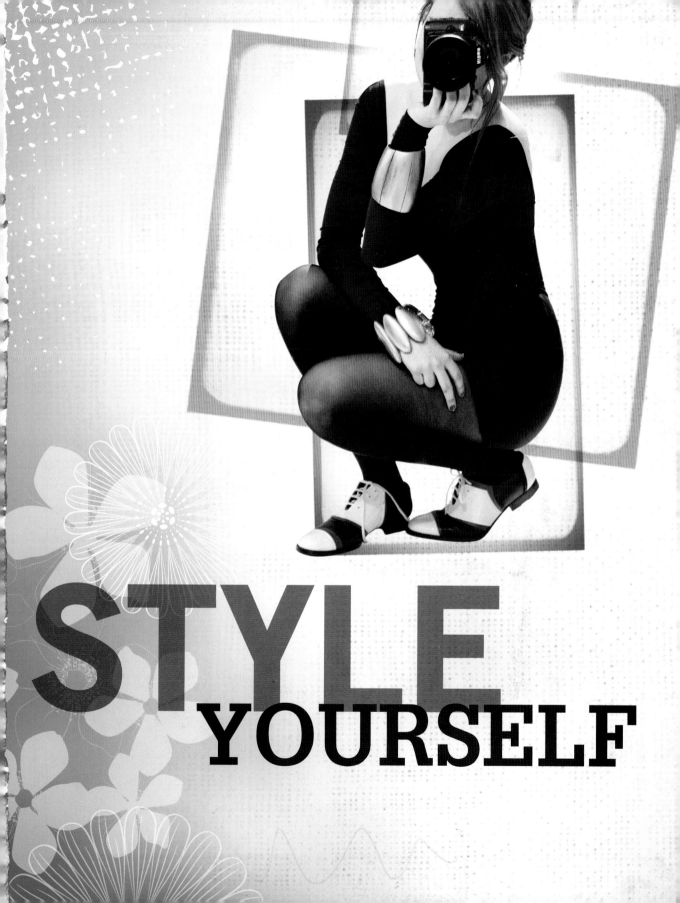

STYLE YOURSELF

STYLE YOURSELF

inspirational advice from the
world's hottest fashion bloggers

APPLE

CONTENTS

A Few Words from
Jane Aldridge | Sea of Shoes

For me, fashion has always been the best form of escapism. When I was three, I dressed up as Coco Chanel for Halloween (my mom, Judy Aldridge, made my costume!), and from then on I was pretty much obsessed with style. I started collecting vintage in Texas thrift stores when I was ten, and by middle school I was usually in trouble for breaking dress code with a pair of over-the-top heels.

Enter the Internet. I started Sea of Shoes in 2007, when I was fifteen. I was bored in the hardcore suburbia just outside of Dallas, and bummed that my friends weren't as fanatical about designer eBay finds as I was. Blogging about my outfits quickly became a way to catalog my inspiration and track my style, and meet other enthusiasts—it was like I'd stumbled upon an online support group for people who love fashion, funny as it sounds! Living in a fashion wasteland must be something a lot of girls can relate to, because all of a sudden my blog had a following.

Now personal-style bloggers are everywhere—reporting on runway shows, showing off their finds, making photocollages of their favorite style icons . . . or just sharing affordable, realistic ways for people to reinvent their wardrobes. And you'll find a ton of those ideas in this book, from bloggers all over the world.

Living in a small community, I had to get resourceful to create my own fantasy fashion world, but I believe that this is something anyone can do, anywhere. My fashion advice to you? Take risks, go for aesthetics that transcend time, and dig deep in unexpected places for items that you love—that inspire you to experiment and express a point of view. When you hit that perfect combo of shape, color, texture, and detail, you'll know you've got it—and that's a pretty rad way to feel.

Jane Aldridge

Nadia Sarwar | Frou Frouu
London, U.K.

Autilia Antonucci
Perth, Australia

Chantal Van Der Meijden | Cocorosa
New York City, U.S.A.

Rhiannon Leifheit | Liebemarlene Vintage
Atlanta, U.S.A.

Here's a quick
glimpse of the many
inspiring fashion
bloggers featured in
Style Yourself . . .
from Johannesburg
to Stockholm,
Atlanta to Osaka.

Michelle Haswell | Kingdom of Style
London, U.K.

Shini Park | Park & Cube
London, U.K.

Tavi Gevinson | Style Rookie
Oak Park, U.S.A.

Funeka Ngwevela | Quirky Stylista
Johannesburg, South Africa

Adeline Rapon
Paris, France

Yuki Lo | Oriental Sunday
Hong Kong, China

Clara Campelo | Zebra T-ash
Rio Branco, Brazil

Shan Shan | Tiny Toadstool
Osaka, Japan

Carolina Engman | Fashion Squad
Stockholm, Sweden

Cristina Morales | La Petite Nymphéa
Barcelona, Spain

Karla Deras | Karla's Closet
Simi Valley, U.S.A.

Susie Lau | Style Bubble
London, U.K.

Barbro Andersen
Oslo, Norway

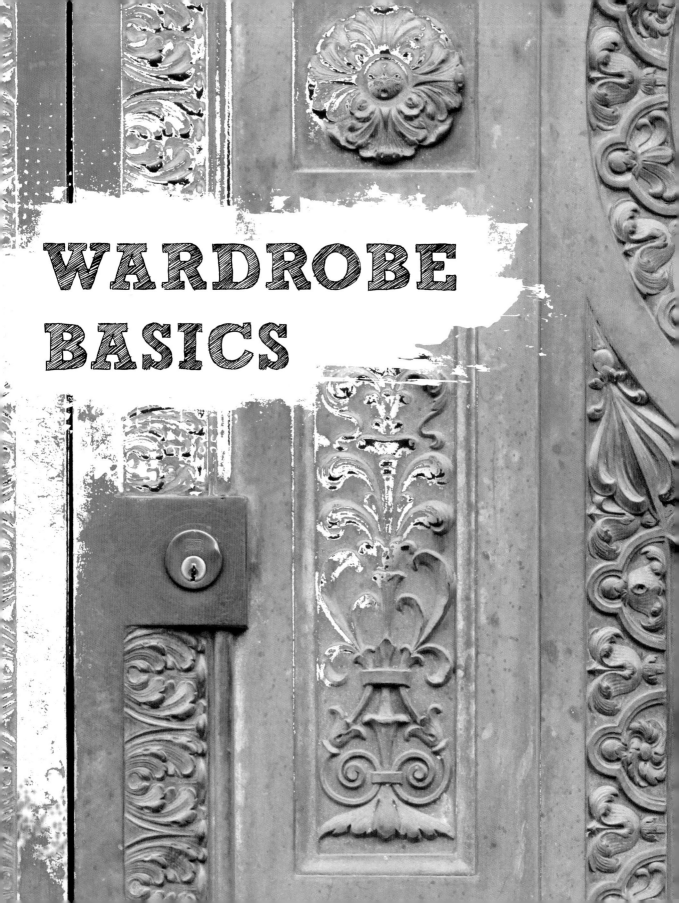

WARDROBE BASICS

BUILD YOUR WARDROBE

There's no hard rule for what garments you should own—after all, your personal style is yours for the making. (Plus, pesky weather and career conditions often make some choices for you.) Still, here are some loose ideas that'll help you ensure you're always covered, whether for a weekend chill-out, a big day at the office, or a smoldering hot date.

TOPS

You can't go wrong with a well-stocked tops drawer—from essentials to fun little extras to full-on outerwear. Don't skimp on tees, even if you live somewhere cold; they're perfect layering solutions.

four basic tees in cuts that flatter you

one basic top with an eye-drawing detail

two long-sleeved tees

two camisoles for layering

three office-friendly shirts

two tops with special touches

two wow-worthy night-out tops

two weekend sweaters

two fitted pullovers

two cardigans in any style

one weather-resistant coat

one winter coat

one office-ready jacket

two weekend jackets

DRESSES

There truly is a dress for every occasion, but more often than not one dress will work in many situations—it's all in the styling. A truly versatile dress can look polished at an interview, cute at a casual afternoon party, and sizzling on a dance floor.

two work-appropriate frocks   three weekend dresses   two party dresses   one superfancy number

BOTTOMS

For most women, the bottom half is hardest to fit just right. So when you find a trouser or jean that makes you look your best, invest in a few colors or washes in the same cut.

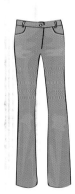

three work pants for various seasons   two Friday-night fun pants   one pair of sleek, classic jeans   one pair of jeans for lounging   one sexy pair

one pair of tailored shorts   one pair of down-and-dirty shorts   two date-night skirts   two weekend skirts   three all-season work skirts

STOCK A FEW ACCESSORIES

Your wardrobe doesn't stop at your closet door—there's also a jewelry box and shoe and purse racks to consider. Since accessories are small, it may be tempting to buy on the fly, which can really add up. But with a little strategy, your outfits will never be without a proper shoe, just-right handbag, or perfect piece of eye-catching jewelry.

SHOES

Shoes have to do hard work—they're what get you uptown, downtown, and all places in between. Have a few comfy get-around shoes, plus a few with heel heights that suit your preferred pant and skirt lengths. Finally, have a few season-appropriate pairs, like strappy summer sandals or heavy-duty rain boots.

two pairs of
go-anywhere
flats

one pair of
sneakers for
errands

one pair of
structured but
low-key shoes

two pairs
of boots, short
or tall

two office-
friendly pumps

one pair of
summertime
sandals

two heels for
formal nights

JEWELRY

It's often the little touches that make an outfit. Start with necklaces that work with your favorite necklines, and stock a few earrings and bracelets that range from dazzling to subtle. Rings are less likely to interfere with a look's overall composition, so it's fine to find a signature one and wear it daily.

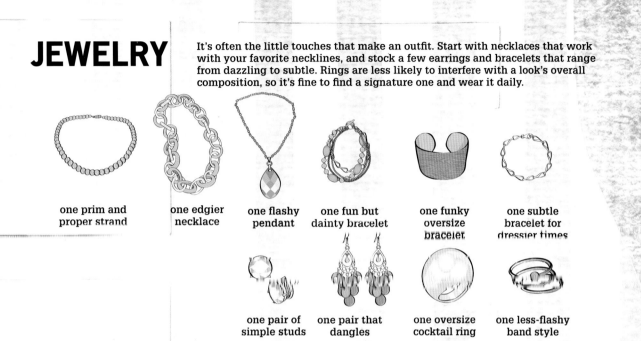

one prim and proper strand

one edgier necklace

one flashy pendant

one fun but dainty bracelet

one funky oversize bracelet

one subtle bracelet for dressier times

one pair of simple studs

one pair that dangles

one oversize cocktail ring

one less-flashy band style

BAGS & BELTS

Bags and belts are utilitarian: They hold stuff, and hold stuff up! If you splurge on one item, make it an everyday satchel that'll keep your look chic. Try wider belts in neutral colors for outfits that require waist definition; stock a colored or textured skinny one for a little extra flair about the waist.

one dressier clutch

one everyday satchel

one casual carry-all tote

one small weekend go bag

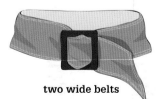

two wide belts

one skinny belt

1

take stock

The best way to launch a whole new you is to start with what you've got. Have a friend over and go through your closet, singling out the garments that make you look and feel your best, and that could be a basis for your updated style. Here, Jazzi and Caroline picked plaid Oxfords in muted tones, vintage-inspired dresses with high waistlines, and ironic cowboy boots as her faves.

BEFORE

BE YOUR OWN STYLIST

. . . with a little help from Jazzi McG!

Even ladies with killer fashion sense sometimes wish for a stylist—a pro who can weed through your wardrobe, demystify what flatters your figure, or source a "wow" look for a special night. Here, stylist and fashion blogger Jazzi McG helps everyday-girl Caroline hit the refresh button on her look, mixing staples from Caroline's closet with some new, trendier pieces fit for her big move to Los Angeles. So follow along and soak up these tricks of the stylist trade, then use them to develop a signature look of your own.

make a plan

Before you hit the mall, know what you need! Caroline's mission called for classroom-friendly duds for her new career as a teacher, plus a few glam looks for going out in a new city. With a slim budget of $150, Jazzi and Caroline hit up Forever 21 for cute, professional separates and vintage megastore Wasteland for pieces with personality.

work-chic results

Caroline's beloved plaid Oxford tops off a new skirt in a slightly off neutral and a long blazer—perfect for hiding those too-cool-for-school tattoos! Brown skimmers and a twisted belt give a scholarly touch.

basking in the L.A. lights

Caroline's love of vintage gets translated into a '50s-style dress with an updated shape and oversize dots, and black velvet booties make her nightlife-ready. A self-made beaded necklace lends personal flair.

AFTER

SHOP SMARTER

You're a bundle of unique features and traits. And no matter your body type, taste, or resources, you can find clothes that make you look and feel amazing, and that you value for their cool, individualistic qualities. Of course, building the ultimate wardrobe takes time and energy (and self-control and honesty). But if you shop thoughtfully, you'll find yourself standing in front of your dream closet.

Take a ruthless inventory.

Make space by donating, gifting, or selling worn-out, ill-fitting, or otherwise not-quite-right stuff. Consider the clothes you own that really work, and jot down their traits—it'll help guide you to more items that are worth your money.

Make a shopping list.

What garments do you always wish you had in your closet? Do you have a big occasion that requires something specific? Those items go at the top of your shopping list.

Stick to your plan.

Stores are designed to push all your impulse buttons. Your list should give you strength to resist unneeded items. That being said, shopping should be fun, so if you fall in love with something that's not on your list, stroll around the block to consider the purchase.

Work with what you've got.

When you're shopping, look for pieces that you could wear with things you already own. If you buy an item needing to source another "perfect something" to make an outfit, that first item will just end up hanging in your closet.

Go ahead—go home empty handed.

Don't cave to the mall's pressures if you don't strike gold; it'll deplete resources that you could spend on an item that you truly love. And resist the lure of the sale rack—if you find a piece that you love on sale, great. But if you wouldn't consider buying it at full price, skip it.

Take others' opinions with a boulder of salt.

Shopping with friends can be a blast. They can inspire you, or urge you to try on surprising items. But no matter how many "oohs" and "aahs" a garment gets, if you aren't thrilled, leave it on the rack.

Decide when to splurge and when to skimp.

If you have a wardrobe hole and you can plug it with a quality item, do it! If you go the cheap-'n'-trendy route, you're likely to have to fill this same hole again each year—which means you'll spend more in the long run. Still, sometimes a flimsy sundress or tee is just what you need. These basics get a lot of wear, so don't feel bad buying a few cheap on-trend versions each year.

Know quality when you see it.

No matter the item, its stitches should be tight and straight (ten stitches per 1 inch/2.5 cm), and a tug at the seams shouldn't make any threads unravel. Buttons should be secure, with stitching around the button holes, and zippers should glide up and down without snagging or creating lumps. If the garment has a pattern, it should line up at the seams. Insider tip: Woven (not printed) labels are a sign of quality.

Be vintage-savvy.

Finding vintage that works with your wardrobe can be quite a hunt, but the rewards are major: You can find pieces that transcend trends and will have a lasting place in your closet. Before you buy, check for weird smells and stains— they probably won't go away—and fabrics that

are stiff or faded, and hold the garment up to the light to check for tears or holes. Special details, like mother of pearl buttons or heavy fabrics with well-anchored decoration, are tell-tale signs of quality.

Jazzi McGilbert | Jazzi McG
Los Angeles, U.S.A.

Hit the virtual mall.

Online shopping is wear it's at—that's where you can hit on amazing deals and one-of-a-kind pieces. But there are some caveats. First, measure yourself and refer to the sizing guides available on most Web sites. (It helps if you've shopped the brand before and know how their sizes run.) Second, read the product description, and use the zoom function. Get in close on a garment to be sure there's no damage (especially if it's vintage) and that you're really thrilled with the print, color, or details. Finally, check the return policy before purchase, and if you're happy with your experience, sign up for newsletters and sale alerts that'll help you snatch up better deals at your favorite sites.

"My clothes are a chance for me to come out of myself, to thrust myself into adventure. While I don't base my outfits on specific paintings, the photos on my blog are like scenes in which I get to be someone else, to play a character."

Louise Ebel | Miss Pandora | Paris, France

TOPS

SHIRT BASICS

You know it when you've found it: a simple and sexy shirt that lets you shine. But a perfect fit can be hard to come by—tailors take over a dozen measurements to craft this wardrobe staple. If you have trouble, choose a shirt that fits in the chest (the trickiest area) and have the rest tailored.

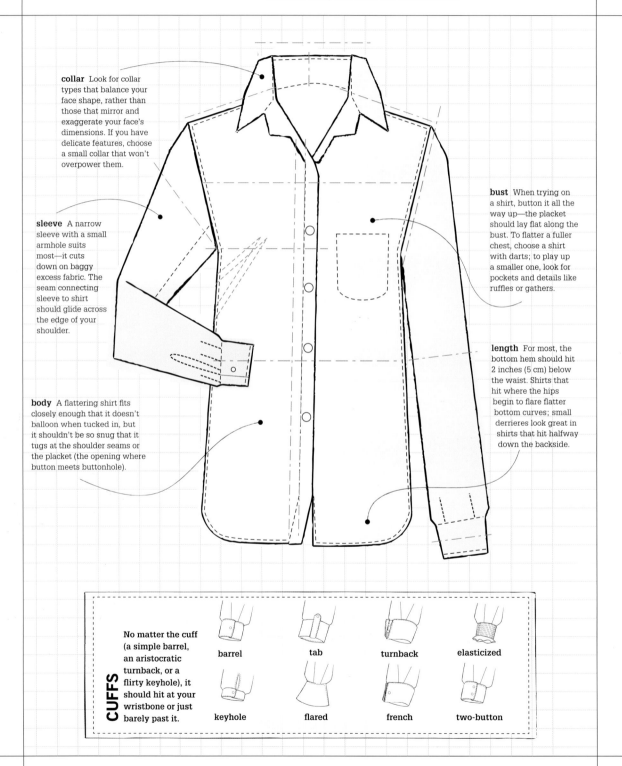

collar Look for collar types that balance your face shape, rather than those that mirror and exaggerate your face's dimensions. If you have delicate features, choose a small collar that won't overpower them.

sleeve A narrow sleeve with a small armhole suits most—it cuts down on baggy excess fabric. The seam connecting sleeve to shirt should glide across the edge of your shoulder.

body A flattering shirt fits closely enough that it doesn't balloon when tucked in, but it shouldn't be so snug that it tugs at the shoulder seams or the placket (the opening where button meets buttonhole).

bust When trying on a shirt, button it all the way up—the placket should lay flat along the bust. To flatter a fuller chest, choose a shirt with darts; to play up a smaller one, look for pockets and details like ruffles or gathers.

length For most, the bottom hem should hit 2 inches (5 cm) below the waist. Shirts that hit where the hips begin to flare flatter bottom curves; small derrieres look great in shirts that hit halfway down the backside.

CUFFS No matter the cuff (a simple barrel, an aristocratic turnback, or a flirty keyhole), it should hit at your wristbone or just barely past it.

barrel

tab

turnback

elasticized

keyhole

flared

french

two-button

crew neck
A circular neckline that fits snug around the base of the neck. Plays up small chests.

v-neck
Hot on everyone. A wide neckline balances out bottom curves; a narrow one is slimming.

polo
The short, pointed collar creates a mix of sporty and preppy, and can make you look taller.

henley
A collarless cousin of the polo, but with playful buttons that let you adjust for a fit that flatters.

split neck
An enticing slice draws eyes down and makes the neck look longer. A tamer v-neck.

boat neck
A neckline that runs from shoulder to shoulder. Long torsos benefit from the horizontal line.

shell
The most basic of sleeveless tops. For a trim shape, seek armholes that cut in on the shoulder.

scoopneck tank
The round dip elongates necks, balances oval faces, and minimizes curves. Magical!

camisole
A graceful tank alternative and a layering must-have. The wide neck flatters most physiques.

cap

elbow

¾-length

bracelet

long

sleeve length
For every arm, there's a perfect sleeve length. Retro ¾-length and elbow sleeves flatter rounder arms, while cap sleeves create shape in slight upper arms.

SHIRTS & BLOUSES
take your pick

Oxford
A tailored classic taken from the guys. Works in casual or formal settings.

roll sleeves
A safari take on the Oxford. Button tabs hold the cuffed sleeves in place.

Western
A snap-shut Oxford with an exaggerated yoke (the piece set in at the shoulders).

knot front
A blouse cut with two shirttails that knot playfully at the waist.

tunic
Longer tunics can also work as mini-dresses. For shape, cinch at the waist.

drawstring
Elastic at the waist creates a billowy drape. Can conceal a thicker middle.

wrap
One side folds over the other and ties. Simplified versions flatter curves.

peasant
Made of light, gathered cotton. Embroidered with bohemian details.

corset
A dramatic bodice made by lines of boning. Can lace up the back or front.

sweetheart neck
A heart-shaped neckline lends tasteful definition to a small bustline.

asymmetrical
An '80s innovation. Pair with classic shapes to keep from overdoing it.

square neck
Frames the face and collarbones. Can counterbalance a long waist.

portrait neck
Open up narrow shoulders with this neckline's wide, arching shape.

jewel neck
A high, rounded neckline with ample coverage. Makes all busts look larger.

mandarin
A short, stand-up collar. Its edges barely meet when the shirt is buttoned.

jabot
Cascading ruffles form a collar. Can be frilly or structured and triangular.

puffed sleeve
Draws the eye upward and creates volume on a slight frame.

balloon sleeve
Very full, ¾-length sleeves with banded cuffs for a full, softly draping shape.

flutter sleeve
Loose, tapered sleeves fall in folds that femme up angular upper arms.

split sleeve
Shoulder-to-wrist slits make this lightweight top unabashedly sexy.

cut-out shoulder
A fresh, modern way to show skin. Comes in slinky or casual fabrics.

tuxedo
The bib front of this evening wear shirt features tiny elegant pintucks.

poet's
Ruffles bring the eye up to the face. Gives volume to small busts.

ascot
A self-tying bow at this blouse's collar gives a nineteenth-century dandy air.

Victorian
A high-collared shirt in delicate, gathered fabric with lace at the neck and cuffs.

Sabrina
A sleeveless play on the boat neck. Adds breadth to slight frames and faces.

keyhole
A modest but flirty oval-shaped hole offers a slight peek at the upper chest.

Peter Pan
Flat collar with rounded ends that lay against the bodice.

middy
This sailor shirt's flat collar extends to the back, making a square "cape."

full round
A fabric band called a stand gives this collar a lift for a tidy, ladylike effect.

plunging
Supersexy; draws the eye down to a glimpse of cleavage. Wear with caution!

halter
Straps meet behind the neck for an open back. Shows off toned shoulders.

tube
A simple tube of clingy fabric. Boning or cups can lend shape and support.

raglan
Sleeves set into the neckline narrow shoulders. A svelte yet sporty shape.

Keiko Groves | Keiko Lynn | Brooklyn, U.S.A

SEQUIN SAFARI

Karla Deras | Karla's Closet | Simi Valley, U.S.A.

all in the mix

I paired this vintage top with a pair of cargo trousers
and Marc Jacobs boots (they're all tattered and scraped;
I've worn these to death!). The cargo trousers offset the
cocktail-style top and make the look more functional.
I added a bag I designed for Coach, plus some glitzy
vintage jewelry—that rhinestone bracelet is actually a
necklace double looped!

Motown mojo

I've always been inspired by the dazzling ladies of Motown music, like the Supremes. Their matching sequin dresses are amazing and incredibly chic—even though these outfits are definitely ritzy, their super-polished, over-the-top look makes me feel brave and inspired enough to incorporate sequined garments into everyday looks. After all, you should always dress to please yourself, not others.

Sometimes a basic shell isn't basic at all—especially when it's encrusted with glittering gold sequins! Wearing sequins in the day is perfectly normal to me, even if I do live in the suburbs where everyone wears running shoes and tee shirts. This look is definitely inspired by Ralph Lauren's spring 2009 collection—I loved how most of the outfits looked as if they had just come from safari, yet the looks were still completely modern and elegant.

dreaming of Morocco

I daydream about meandering through the alleys and archways of Morocco in this outfit. There's something so romantic about Tangier, with its arched walkways and desert-meets-sea views. This outfit's colors seem just right for it!

ROCKER TEE REMIX

Band tees aren't just for concerts. You've been collecting these babies for years and they may be a little worn, but they can show off an adventurous taste in music and lend humor and contrast to any look. Go glam rock on sexy nights out, make it flirty and skirty for casual dates, or opt for low-key layers when running basic errands.

Charlene O'Rourke | s.t.r.u.t.t.
London, U.K.

metal maiden
"This Slayer shirt was my boyfriend's but slowly found its way into my wardrobe. I wanted to look dressier, so I added glamorous hair and makeup to the rebellious tee, thigh highs, and shoes."

rock 'n' roll ballerina

"I instantly knew my boyfriend's Pink Floyd tee had to be incorporated into a look. It contrasts perfectly with my girly pink skirt and the bows on my heels—I adore the juxtaposition of masculine and feminine."

living on a layer

"This Bon Jovi tee shirt belongs to my dad; he is a huge fan. I love styling items differently than how they're supposed to be worn, like my randomly buttoned cardigan and tuxedo blazer."

SWEATERS
take your pick

twinset
Two layers that were made for each other! Pair with less prim accessories.

cardigan
Front buttons and tons of shapes mean endless styling variations.

long cardigan
Doubles as a light fall jacket and warm under-coat layer for wintertime.

cropped cardigan
Pick special colors or textures that might overwhelm in a bulkier sweater.

open-front cardigan
Without a front closure, this sweater can be belted, tied, or left open and drapey.

waterfall cardigan
An open front cascades down in architectural folds. Try it over a simple tee.

vest
A knit vest adds an uptown and sassy vibe to basic business wear.

scarf
The attached scarf in matching fabric keeps it cozy but not too busy.

shrug
A cute, cropped shape covers just the arms and the upper back.

caped
Add volume to a small frame with this top's fluttery layer at the neck.

shawl
A wide collar with long, rounded lapels feels casual and fireside-toasty.

cowl
Highlights the collarbones and drapes nicely over a full bust.

hoodie
A soft hood with a drawstring closure. Posh fabrics update this slacker staple.

zip front
A sporty option that's classier than a sweatshirt on the weekends.

off the shoulder
The name says it all. This coquettish top is flattering to fuller bustlines.

ruched
Gathered seams nip for a pretty shape and bust-enhancing, rippled details.

batwing sleeve
Large armholes extend almost to the waist for ample arm coverage.

bell sleeve
Sleeves flare out from the shoulder. Balances a large bust or upper arms.

pullover
Whether crew- or v-neck, an indispensable wardrobe staple.

boyfriend
Try a slouchy v-neck sweater and knit scarf for boyish, low-key appeal.

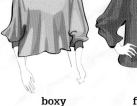

boxy
Pair a short, roomy sweater with skinny pants for a sexy contrast in shape.

fisherman
A traditional Irish knit made of undyed wool and featuring textural patterns.

uneven hem
A deliberately jagged hemline modernizes a basic look. Best for longer torsos.

banded waist
A stretchy, fitted hem allows this top to blouse—perfect camo for a tummy.

pinup
Coyly snug with a Peter Pan collar and short sleeves. A wink to the flirty '50s.

twist front
Knit fabric is draped across and sewn into place for an artistic touch.

funnel neck
A turtleneck plus! Extra fabric warms the neck and brings eyes up to the face.

roll neck
An easy, outdoorsy look with edges that are cut and rolled instead of hemmed.

turtleneck
A high, close-fitting collar that folds over on itself. Elongates petite frames.

mock neck
A short, one-layer collar that doesn't fold over. Flatters round, wide faces.

bishop sleeve
The cuff edge is gathered with elastic so the sleeve gently balloons.

dolman
Wide armholes narrow through the forearm, forming a triangular sleeve.

mutton sleeve
A sleeve that puffs at the shoulder and is fitted from the elbow down.

"When I wear this vintage sweater, I feel like I'm in the good ole days, when a gal could play dominoes by the fireplace with her favorite record spinning in the living room and be content."

Whitney Williams | A la Ladywolf
Jonesborough, U.S.A.

CARDIGAN REMIX

Your old gray cardigan doesn't have to be boring anymore. It's all about how you style and accessorize! A colorful brooch here, a funky belt there, and soon you'll find new ways to pair that cardi with items you already own and elevate your look from dull to darling.

multilayered
Use it under other tops to turn your outfit into a superchic, structured masterpiece.

wrapped with a brooch
Create curves and add sparkle by wrapping and pinning with a fun brooch or two.

twisted as a scarf
Take the sleeves and drape the cardi around your neck artfully, then pin it in place.

cardigan
Don't underestimate this wardrobe staple and key layering tool. Feel free to own many—from cropped to long, neutral to bright, fitted to boxy. Use it to keep warm and complete your look.

backward and belted
Go unexpected by flipping that cardi around. Add a necklace to avoid a plain front.

open with a belt
A belt trims your waist and adds a trendy touch—polished fashion for the office.

open and tucked
For a sleek line, wear a silky or Victorian top under your cardi, then tuck both into pants.

GRUNGE GAMINE

Adeline Rapon | Paris, France

Oversize sweaters are my leitmotif in winter; I just like the big shape of them. But the problem is not looking like a trucker—that's why I wore this one with shorts and wool tights to show off my legs. When I look at this photo, I can see that I was having a really good time. This is the outfit to wear when you're out playing in the snow with a great friend.

Palais de Tokyo

I wore this look when it was horribly cold, but staying at home seemed so terribly boring. Paris is full of chances to get out—there are lots of museums and exhibitions. So, on this day, I went with a friend to the Palais de Tokyo, a museum that always has weird happenings and stays open late. I carried this bag, which I guess is kind of like art—my friend's girlfriend designed it, and it's got all these photos of people making crazy faces.

laissez-faire mode

Here I'm wearing two sweaters, both in big wool, both from the Gap. The socks and boots match the colors in the sweaters, but I don't even think that was on purpose. And when it's snowy out, I can't wear anything but Doc Martens; otherwise my feet freeze and I fall a lot. The key I'm wearing on a plain chain goes to a room in my house but I don't know which one, so it's more useful this way. And I love this knit hat—it makes me look like a pixie.

'90s throwback

I call this look *lutin des neiges*—it means snow goblin—because the look is impish and gritty. I was inspired by grunge artists like Kurt Cobain and by '90s fashion, and so this look is all very masculine: the Docs, the big sweater, and even the bag.

Lutin des neiges

OUTERWEAR BASICS

Coat shopping isn't the time to go wild with seasonal trends or over-the-top novelty. A nice coat may be pricey, but if you choose a style that will endure, a fit that flatters, and a color that works with your wardrobe's palette, you'll stay in love with it—winter after winter.

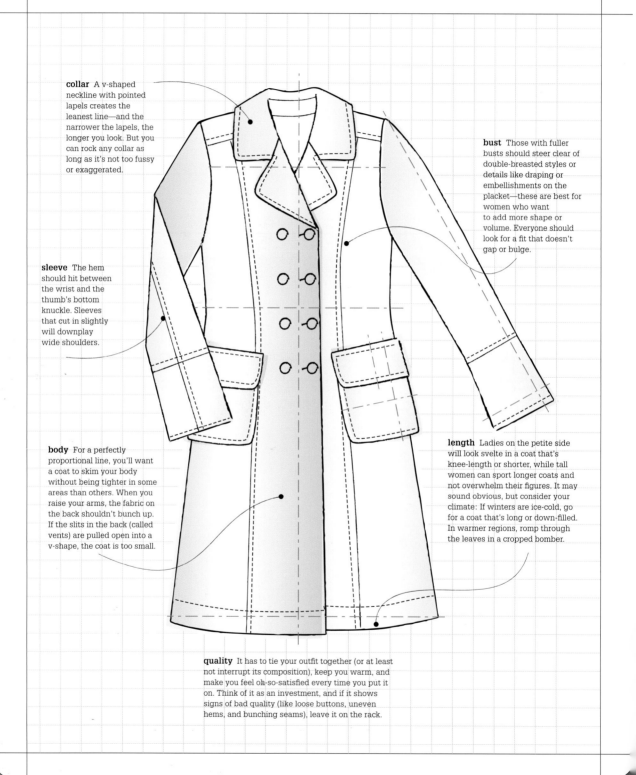

collar A v-shaped neckline with pointed lapels creates the leanest line—and the narrower the lapels, the longer you look. But you can rock any collar as long as it's not too fussy or exaggerated.

bust Those with fuller busts should steer clear of double-breasted styles or details like draping or embellishments on the placket—these are best for women who want to add more shape or volume. Everyone should look for a fit that doesn't gap or bulge.

sleeve The hem should hit between the wrist and the thumb's bottom knuckle. Sleeves that cut in slightly will downplay wide shoulders.

body For a perfectly proportional line, you'll want a coat to skim your body without being tighter in some areas than others. When you raise your arms, the fabric on the back shouldn't bunch up. If the slits in the back (called vents) are pulled open into a v-shape, the coat is too small.

length Ladies on the petite side will look svelte in a coat that's knee-length or shorter, while tall women can sport longer coats and not overwhelm their figures. It may sound obvious, but consider your climate: If winters are ice-cold, go for a coat that's long or down-filled. In warmer regions, romp through the leaves in a cropped bomber.

quality It has to tie your outfit together (or at least not interrupt its composition), keep you warm, and make you feel oh-so-satisfied every time you put it on. Think of it as an investment, and if it shows signs of bad quality (like loose buttons, uneven hems, and bunching seams), leave it on the rack.

shell
Get a little shimmer with this button's subtle flashes of iridescent color.

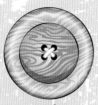

wooden
The natural color and grain give any outfit an organic, earthy feel.

nautical
Often spotted lending a maritime feel to peacoats. Usually in brass or plastic.

military
Find these insignia-marked metal buttons on a double-breasted garment.

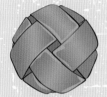

leather knot
Braided strips of leather create a textured dome shape and a cozy vibe.

covered
This refined button is made of the same fabric as the coat that it fastens.

carved
A recessed pattern is a vintage treat, especially on bright, oversize buttons.

frog
A Chinese-inspired ornamental closure made of silk ribbon or cord.

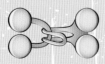

hook and eye
From corsets to coats, these tiny closures are minimal but sexy.

toggle
Sailor-chic! Made of horn and leather and easy to undo, even in thick gloves.

coat fasteners
If you don't dig a coat's buttons, shop for some you love and switch them out. You can also mount button backs on jewelry or other tiny objects for a more personalized feel.

Ebba Zingmark | Ebba Foton | Umea, Sweden

JACKETS
take your pick

waistcoat
In pinstripes or polka dots, it strikes a fun tone. Draws the eye to the chest.

gilet
A sleeveless topper is perfect over a sweater when it's too warm for a coat.

cape
A striking silhouette that envelops the body. Try belting it if it's too expansive.

moto
Often in sexy but protective leather. Diagonal zippers make dynamic lines.

bomber
Inspired by fighter pilots. Features supple leather and knit trim.

denim
A straight shape that hits at the hip. To go romantic, layer over floaty dresses.

field
A counterculture symbol from the '60s. Wear it open over fitted shapes.

utility
Features plenty of pockets, a hood, and a warm (sometimes removable) lining.

equestrian
A slim line often with leather details. Take it from the trail to the office.

casual
Wide lapels and a cropped, youthful shape. Try in velvet or seersucker.

summer blazer
Get a polished look in warmer months by wearing a sweet short-sleeved blazer.

double-breasted
Try wearing a long, schoolboy-inspired blazer over a floral or flirty dress.

one-button
The single-button closure creates a blazer with a body-skimming fit.

three-button
A blazer with three buttons is typically shorter, boxier, and more casual.

hooded vest
Keeps your core warm when sleeves get in the way. Often down-filled.

bolero
A short, structured jacket originally worn on formal occasions.

zouave
With a curved, open front and full sleeves. Trimmed with braiding.

cropped
Hits above the hips to show off a nice midzone. Pair with high-waisted pants.

bed jacket
Take lacy retro lingerie to the street by sassing it up with jeans or boots.

capelet
A short cape drapes over the arms and fastens in front to cut an evening chill.

letterman
A combination of wool and leather. With scholastic patches and colors.

peplum
An attached flounce adds curve to the hips. Popularized in the 1940s.

collarless
A minimal silhouette doesn't distract from small faces or delicate features.

quilted
Usually a boxy shape. Two layers of fabric have warm padding in between.

blouson
Hits at the hip with a ribbed and elasticized hem. Nips in the waist.

drawstring
Oversize hoods and other design details give personality to a casual piece.

belted
A belt lets you adjust the waistline to find your own most flattering fit.

swing
This jacket's gentle flare and ¾-length sleeves give it girlish whimsy.

drape front
Extra fabric falls elegantly instead of a collar. Try it in luscious leather.

fringed
Edged in suede strips. Cowboy flair and rocker swagger in one sexy jacket.

windbreaker
Lightweight and impermeable. A top layer for warm rain or exercise.

track
With a stand-up collar and usually contrasting stripes on the arms.

matching the landscape
This mustard silk scarf is one of my most versatile accessories. In this case, to suit the playful and charming nature of the outfit, I tied the scarf in a bow and tucked it under my collar. What I really like is how well its colors complement the Karratha scenery, as do the red- and straw-browns in the satchel, belt, and clogs.

build your look

Prim & Proper Trailblazer

Autilia Antonucci | Perth, Australia

I was visiting my parents in the sunny town of Karratha in Northwest Australia when I wore this look. I borrowed the white lace blazer from my sister and added a paisley scarf and pearls, then I tacked on nautical stripes, sturdy clogs, and a straw boater hat to make the look equal parts refined schoolgirl and outback sporting. Then we went on a jaunt to take some photos!

les scènes du cinéma

I love old classic movies and sometimes wonder if I subconsciously created this look with a scene from *Roman Holiday* in mind. In this outfit I feel as if I could step into Audrey Hepburn's shoes and fly around Rome on a scooter with Gregory Peck quite easily! The pale palette, lacy textures, and uniform-inspired pieces also remind me of the feminine but jaunt-ready costumes in *Picnic at Hanging Rock*, a 1975 film about Australian schoolgirls who disappear after exploring a rock formation in the countryside. (My sister and I made it back just fine from our walk, though, don't worry!)

traditional versus trendy

Fashion is far more interesting when you push the boundaries. In this outfit I tried to balance controversial trends with standard staples. For instance, the cropped blazer shape is pretty current, but pearls and lace are always around. Sandals over socks are very trendy right now (and for some people, this look only calls to mind images of their grandpa sitting on the front porch!), but stripes seem to always work. It's all in the balance.

CAPE
REMIX

Whether you're going for superhero playfulness or opera-ready melodrama, a cape is a light jacket with ample coverage, which makes it great for in-between seasons. Make your cape the center of attention by drawing it shut over slouchy black bottoms; drape it nonchalantly over streetwear for carefree elegance; or let it frame tailored shorts for a fun, cheeky look.

Nadia Sarwar | Frou Frouu
London, U.K.

shuttering out the rain
"It was a horribly rainy day so I threw the cape over everything and it became the look's focal point. The droopy trousers and sandals over socks make the look modern and eclectic."

Sandra Hagelstam | 5 Inch and Up
London, U.K.

ahead of the class
"This is just a casual everyday outfit—I tossed the cape over motorcycle-inspired jeans and a loose blouse on my way to university. I wanted to dress in shades of beige for spring."

Giselle Chapman | Style of a Fashionista
Guildford, U.K.

the long and short of it
"I totally fell for the oversize-cape-with-shorts idea. This was a great transitional look that I wore on a warm spring day for a spot of shopping and lunch with friends."

COATS
take your pick

car
A short-collared coat that hits midthigh. Add a silk scarf and go for a drive!

walking
Falls near the knee. The versatile A-line shape can work over any outfit.

funnel
The stand-up collar looks modern and blocks wind—no need for a scarf.

wrap
A drapey shape that's belted offers figure-flattering waist definition.

opera
Complement a lavish outfit with a sophisticated topper in velvet or silk.

swagger
A ladylike '30s style with a swingy shape that can conceal a tummy or wide hips.

fur
Adds a luxe touch to basics like jeans. Seek out vintage or synthetic versions.

camel
A stately golden-brown coat made of camel hair, which has a subtle texture.

shearling
Sheep- or lambskin is shorn and fashioned into cozy, luxurious pieces.

parka
Often includes a fur-lined hood and long length to protect from cold.

duffle
A comfy shape in wool with a hood, toggles, and roomy patch pockets.

puffy down
Channels between layers of fabric are stuffed with down for ultimate warmth.

ski
With snowproof fabric, insulation, and a storm flap over the zipper. Sporty!

overcoat
A long, chic coat that covers the legs. Flatters tall ladies; try in a bold color.

peacoat
A look taken from sailors. Double-breasted with wide, notched lapels.

side-button
Asymmetrical closures can help de-emphasize bulk on larger figures.

tailcoat
Be fancy but quirky with a style stolen from men's formal tuxedos.

military
Featuring details like epaulettes, this fierce style is best in a fitted silhouette.

sweater
Thickly knit wool can elevate the cardigan concept. Cozy and insulating.

cocoon
An easy-to-wear, voluminous shape that envelops you with warmth.

poncho
Drapes over the body with a hole for the head. Modernize with a sleek pant.

cloak
A floor-length garment with a front closure and a dose of fairy-tale drama.

blanket
Oversize and made of thick, woven fabric, often in a graphic pattern.

trench
Made for drizzle but always stylish. With a rain shield, gun flap, and D-ring belt.

bubble raincoat
A drawstring around the bottom hem can be cinched for more shape.

macintosh
Made of special plastic-coated fabric invented for keeping dry on rainy days.

duster
A light topper with a slit up the back for straddling a horse (or scooter!).

Alice Point | Krakow, Poland

pretty chaos

There's a lot going on in this look, and that's just the way I like it—the secret is in balancing all the colors and shapes! Here, the coat's bright blue and orange colors pop up again in the dress's bright print, and the gloves and necklace rock the same black-and-gold theme. Plus, the shapes in the jewelry and garments all play off each other—see all those triangles and rectangles in the fur collar, the studs on the gloves, and the messy geometric floral? They make for a glamorously choppy and hard-edged look. There! That's how I do it.

build your look

SHE WORE BLUE VELVET

Kelly Framel | The Glamourai | Brooklyn, U.S.A.

I don't do outfits—I do costumes. For me, every day is a chance to wear something decadent but never over-the-top. I built this look around a bold blue vintage coat that I revamped with fur and other finery, and then I edged out its classic frumpiness with tough-girl accessories.

DIY maven

I stumbled across this cobalt cotton-velour wonder in a vintage store in Pittsburgh and just had to have it! But it needed a little Glamourai touch. For the cuffs, I cut up an old belt found on eBay, and I topped off the coat with a red fox collar (a score from another late-night eBay binge). As for accessories, I added oversize gold studs to fingerless gloves that I picked up in a biker shop, and I designed and made the chain necklace myself.

ELEMENTS OF STYLE ACCORDING TO
IRIS APFEL:

1 Never take yourself or an outfit too seriously

2 Visit the animal kingdom

3 Consider the clergy

4 Travel widely

5 Go high and low

6 Don't fret about your age

7 Don't be afraid to stop traffic

Palm Beach eccentric

I love to dress the way a half-mad grandmother might, if trapped in a young woman's body. So for me, fashion icon Iris Apfel is one of the greatest dressers of all time. She has inimitable style and happily ignores preconceptions of what is fashionable. I constantly draw on her whimsical aesthetic, but modernize it with restrained rebellion: sexy black hosiery, very high heels, ferocious studded gloves, and a stacked bob haircut.

"Whenever I put together **menswear-inspired** outfits, I always end up throwing in something **romantic**. This button up shirt, trench, and boots combination was so **tomboy** that I had to tie a ribbon in my hair to make it a little more me."

Rhiannon Leifheit | Liebemarlene Vintage | Atlanta, U.S.A.

TRENCHES

This smart staple is timeless and a weatherproof must in any wardrobe. Plus, it's superversatile! You can exude modern elegance by turning it into a wrap dress, or give a flash of peekaboo blue by leaving it open but belted. Or layer it with bright leggings and an oversize black cardigan for a warm look with lots of dimension.

June Paski | Bandung, Indonesia

Alice Point | Krakow, Poland

Meijia Shao | Fashion Is My Life
Shanghai, China

Liz Cherkasova | Late Afternoon
San Francisco, U.S.A.

Golestaneh Koochak Poor | Golestaneh Street Style
Cologne, Germany

Karla Deras | Karla's Closet
Simi Valley, U.S.A.

BOTTOMS

PANTS BASICS

Katharine Hepburn nailed nonchalant elegance with her crisp, menswear-inspired trousers in the 1930s. And with a little fit savvy, you can wear the same oh-so-chic shape. Before hitting the dressing room, know your waist and inseam measurements, and load up on a range of sizes, as they vary between designers.

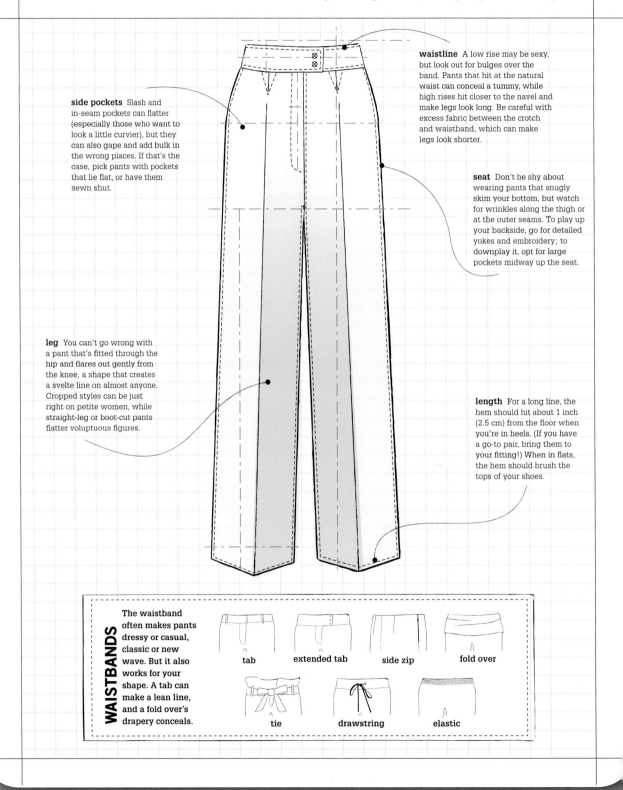

side pockets Slash and in-seam pockets can flatter (especially those who want to look a little curvier), but they can also gape and add bulk in the wrong places. If that's the case, pick pants with pockets that lie flat, or have them sewn shut.

waistline A low rise may be sexy, but look out for bulges over the band. Pants that hit at the natural waist can conceal a tummy, while high rises hit closer to the navel and make legs look long. Be careful with excess fabric between the crotch and waistband, which can make legs look shorter.

seat Don't be shy about wearing pants that snugly skim your bottom, but watch for wrinkles along the thigh or at the outer seams. To play up your backside, go for detailed yokes and embroidery; to downplay it, opt for large pockets midway up the seat.

leg You can't go wrong with a pant that's fitted through the hip and flares out gently from the knee, a shape that creates a svelte line on almost anyone. Cropped styles can be just right on petite women, while straight-leg or boot-cut pants flatter voluptuous figures.

length For a long line, the hem should hit about 1 inch (2.5 cm) from the floor when you're in heels. (If you have a go-to pair, bring them to your fitting!) When in flats, the hem should brush the tops of your shoes.

WAISTBANDS

The waistband often makes pants dressy or casual, classic or new wave. But it also works for your shape. A tab can make a lean line, and a fold over's drapery conceals.

tab

extended tab

side zip

fold over

tie

drawstring

elastic

cargo
Expands to fit more than the average pocket does. May be a bit bulky.

pant length
You can go daringly short, graceful and floor-skimming, or cutely cropped. But in general, the best hem hits (and emphasizes) a pretty point in your leg's shape.

in-seam
A pouch sewn in right at the side seam. Sneaky, but not a lot of storage space.

slash
A pouch slanting down to the outer leg. Can create a smooth front over a tummy.

rounded
A flat, flattering pocket on the front hip of casual pants. Rarely gapes or bulges.

coin
A tiny accent most often found on jeans. First used to carry pocket watches.

patch
A pouch sewn on the outside of a garment. Can come in many shapes and sizes.

flap
A patch pocket with a utilitarian closure. Gives a little extra oomph to small behinds.

welt
A slit allows access to a pouch in the lining. Often edged with different fabric.

zip
A zipper keeps lining tucked inside a welt pocket, making a clean shape.

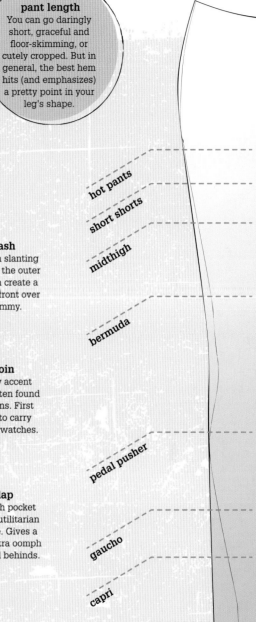

hot pants

short shorts

midthigh

bermuda

pedal pusher

gaucho

capri

ankle

classic

PANTS
take your pick

basic trouser
An office staple that hits at the natural waist. Crease in front for a long line.

pleated
Figure-friendly pleats add extra room, but lay flat when you stand.

cuffed
A playful cuff suits straight, narrow bodies. Add slim heels for height.

yoga
An exercise favorite of stretchy fabric. Also spotted as a casual pant.

sash
A fabric belt that ties adds femininity and updates the typical trouser.

palazzo
Loose pants in flowy fabrics flatter full thighs. Balance with a fitted top.

pajama
Dress up a sexy, silky version of this loungewear favorite with strappy heels.

gaucho
This Spanish twist on the capri flares below the knee. Pair with high boots.

capri
A snug, casual pant made popular in the '50s. Hits midcalf or below the calf.

balloon
Wide to the ankle, then gathered with a band. Often in airy, gauzy fabrics.

evening
Elegant pants that drape gracefully over fuller hips. Try in crepe or silk.

carrot
Fuller through the hips and tapering at the ankle. Gives shape to small hips.

harem
Eastern-inspired trousers with a dropped crotch. Keep it sleek on top.

parachute
Tapered pants made of ripstop nylon (parachute fabric) with tons of zippers.

riding
A suede or leather inner knee patch stands up to friction against the saddle.

menswear
A slouchier, more masculine trouser. Often features cuffs and pleats.

chino
Smart, preppy pants made of cotton twill. Often straight-leg and low-rise.

sailor
High-waisted, flared, and slimming pants with buttons on the front flap.

Zanita Whittington | Sydney, Australia

pedal pusher
Originally worn by cyclists. Similar to the capri, but hits higher for mobility.

cargo
Highly functional pants with utility pockets. Seek out sleeker versions.

jodhpur
Full from the hip to the knee, then tapers. First popular with British cavalry.

cigarette
A narrow, straight, and ankle-length pant. More polished than skinny jeans.

leggings
First worn in the cold as underwear. Perfect under dresses or tunics.

stirrup
Formfitting leggings that secure with a stretchy band around the instep.

suspender
Boyish pants with detachable straps that are made from matching fabric.

jumpsuit
Parachutists first sported these on the job. Look for feminine shapes.

catsuit
A daring one-piece that fits tight across curves and makes a feline silhouette.

"Isn't it ironic that it's the **simplest outfit** you feel **most confident** in? There's something about carrying a quirky canvas tote instead of a purse, or wearing a basic gray tee . . . it's like **rolling up your sleeves** and getting ready to enjoy the day."

Shini Park | Park & Cube | London, U.K.

CAPRI PANT REMIX

These cute cropped trousers can be hard to rock. But be brave! Try them in a bright color, then build looks that stress long lines and provide texture, pattern, or pops of color that draw the eye up—whether belted with a tunic, tucked in to make curves, or high-waisted like a 1950s pinup star.

Karla Deras | Karla's Closet
Simi Valley, U.S.A.

it's a cinch
"I belted my felt polka-dot jacket and added funky leopard ankle boots and retro shades, plus a chunky crystal bracelet gifted to me by my boyfriend. Edgy and elegant all at once."

ladylike with lace
"This outfit is definitely very girly with the vintage multistrand pearl necklace and lace top paired with slingback heels. I'd probably wear this to do some shopping with my friends!"

high-waisted & high-stepping
"This look would be perfect for running errands or sitting at a cafe. I tied up a men's silk patterned shirt to wear with a custom-fit Levi's jacket, large tote bag, and platform sandals."

build your look

A Cloud in Trousers

Shini Park | Park & Cube | London, U.K.

I fell in love with these tapered Vero Moda pants for the pattern—it reminded me of a cloud-scattered pastel sky during dawn, which is possibly why I paired it with pastel-toned lace and chunky knits. I felt like I was in my pajamas the entire day!

maker spirit

On the day I wore this outfit I went to an exhibit where the rooms were like sketchbooks, spilling out onto walls and floors—paper mobiles, collages, murals. I'm a designer and am really drawn to creative spaces and projects. I think part of the reason I like these pants is because they remind me of a DIY project from a few months back, when I bleached a pair of tights and embellished them with pearls.

sweet inspiration

I love how these pegleg pants sit so naturally on my waist and give my legs room to breathe. For this outfit I think I wanted to imitate a shape of an ice-cream cone so I added a big wool scarf on top, and finished with narrow cookie-colored wedges.

a day at Brighton Beach

This outfit was put together by my inner child. Notice the double braids and the pastels! I feel like with the clown behind me, there's a seaside carnival atmosphere to this look—like I'm at Brighton Beach. I usually have an irrational fear of clowns, but posing with this one suited my outfit's mood.

JEANS
take your pick

straight
The iconic, original fit that's always a laidback but sexy style statement.

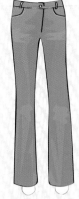

boot cut
A slight flare from the knee glides over shoes for a long, lean look on anyone.

wide leg
Flares from the hips for an easy fit all the way down. Masks larger thighs.

flared
Narrow to the knee, then flares to balance curvier upper bodies.

trouser
Slash pockets, an extended tab, and a front crease make for dressier denim.

bell bottom
Fitted through the thigh with extra flare from the knee for '70s swagger.

boyfriend
A roomy, straight fit often with a low rise. Best for tall and narrow frames.

carpenter
With workwear-inspired details like hammer loops and utility pockets.

high-waisted
Elongates petite legs and creates a smooth shape to accentuate curves.

skinny
Snugly fitted to every curve, from hip to ankle. Try with slouchy tops.

jeggings
A modern, minimal, and slimmer-than-slim version made from stretch denim.

moto
Extra seams around the knees imitate motorcycle gear's tough look.

overalls
A playful and utilitarian one-piece with adjustable, snap-close straps.

Denim Treatments

Denim is a cotton twill made up of indigo thread woven across white filler thread, with results ranging from a tidy diagonal pattern to a rugged, broken zigzag. A wide array of washes and treatments lets you choose what to exude—from dark and crisp to weathered and easygoing to nearly destroyed.

classic
A clean, medium indigo wash that works with everything in your closet and is always in demand.

stonewashed
Denim takes a tumble with pumice stones, which roughen up the fabric for an overall worn-in look.

antique
Denim that's produced on vintage-style looms has a handmade quality and unique texture.

bio-stonewashing
Enzymes are harnessed to eat away at outer fibers and dyes, displaying the white filler color under the indigo.

raw
Not washed after dyeing, this denim starts dark and stiff, fading as it's worn for a personalized appearance.

chemical
Bleach is used to fade denim for a special, pale color, while acid washes are achieved with chlorine-soaked pumice stones.

dirty
Manufacturers get a "dirty" effect by dyeing the filler thread a yellowish tint. When woven with indigo, this yellow peeks through.

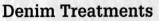

forever in blue jeans
DENIM

Jeans—they're the ultimate populist pant. From boutique designs to styles that do hard labor, denim has a place in everyone's closet. With tons of cuts (go baggy but cuffed, or surprise with a romper) and a wealth of rinses (try a nasty but nice acid wash), it's no wonder Yves Saint-Laurent wished he'd invented them first. And jeans look better the more they're worn—getting that faded, worn-in look that means love.

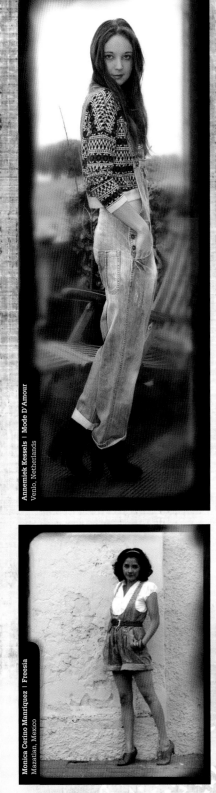

Annemiek Kessels | Mode D'Amour
Venlo, Netherlands

Jane Aldridge | Sea of Shoes
Dallas, U.S.A.

Jessica Virgin | Vintage Virgin
Montrose, U.S.A.

Eszter Farkas | Stylorectic
Vienna, Austria

Monica Cerino Manriquez | Freesia
Mazatlan, Mexico

Sonu Bohra | Fashion Bombay
Mumbai, India

bermuda
A summer vacation staple that hits just above the knee. Great on long legs.

knickers
Not just for golf. Elevated by refined pairings, they can be daringly chic.

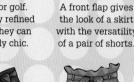

skort
A front flap gives the look of a skirt with the versatility of a pair of shorts.

yoked
Define your middle with a seamed section around the waist and hips.

scalloped
A delicate edge completes a breezy form. Draws the eye to nice thighs.

petal
Curved layers meet in front and add dimension and shape to thin legs.

culottes
A wide, yoked short sits on the natural waist and is cut to look like a skirt.

sash
Forgo a fussy belt in the heat with a sash tie made of the shorts' fabric.

paper bag
Gathered volume in the waist adds curves to a thin or slight frame.

belted
A complementary belt trims the waist and looks casually put-together.

lounge
A drawstring cinches casual knit shorts that go from couch to gym.

track
Made of breathable fabrics. Often with bright colors and contrasting stripes.

tailored
A well-shaped, medium-length short with cuffs can elongate legs.

newsie
Straight and cuffed. Pair with lace-up booties for boyish Victorian charm.

pinup
The sassy sailor-style front makes petite women look longer.

chino
Rugged cotton fabric looks crisp and neat but holds up to playtime, too.

short
An ultrasexy, iconic style that exudes courage. A relaxed fit keeps it classy.

hot pants
A bare-minimum disco style. Glam it up and be prepared for stares!

SHORTS
take your pick

camp
Fully equipped with patch pockets. Add a canvas belt for bonus scout appeal.

side tie
A tie at each outside hem gives this pair a dainty, flirty touch.

bloomers
Gathered with a band at the bottom hem. A cheeky vintage style.

bubble
Extra volume and a drawn-in hem slim legs and create a quirky silhouette.

draped
A bold option in slinky fabrics with oversize, graceful drop pockets.

cycle
A snug, stretchy pair stolen from sports gear. Try it under a minidress.

board
Quick-drying fabric and a drawstring make these ideal for hitting the surf.

fold over
The waistband doubles down for a sexy touch, adding curves to the hips.

tap
A supershort and frisky pair usually made of floaty silk, satin, or lace.

denim cutoffs
A no-brainer in hot summer. Cut up old jeans, or buy a pre-frayed pair.

boyfriend denim
A longer, slouchy-fitting denim short. Pair with heels for a sassy contrast.

roll up
Side tabs button so you can adjust for a flattering length or specific occasions.

surplus
Expandable pockets and a grommet belt prep you for fashion battle—or a hike.

cargo
Seriously functional with pockets along the outer seam and a straight fit.

romper
A playful one-piece. Requires a pristine fit through the crotch and backside.

Alice Point | Krakow, Poland

SHORTS REMIX

Crisply tailored with a flirty detail at the hem, these scallop-edged shorts aren't your old gym uniform—and they can go just about anywhere. For office-ready finesse, pair them with a blazer, wide belt, and nude pumps. If it's cozy chic you're after, keep it simple with a slouchy sweater and T-strap flats. To segue into cool times and keep it sharp, wear with tights and chunky jewelry.

Keiko Groves | Keiko Lynn
Brooklyn, U.S.A.

at a desk by the seashore
"The name of the shorts ('Lovely Wave') put me in a nautical state of mind. I paired them with navy stripes and gold hardware. Even the necklace reminds me of a ship's wheel!"

couch potato cutie
"Frumpy frumpy, but oh-so-comfy. Though this look was all about comfort, I love the way the soft pink pairs with the vintage feel of the studded T-straps and the customized locket."

big night out
"When the weather gets a little chilly, I layer tights beneath my favorite shorts. High-heeled booties and a statement necklace are just enough to dress it up and lend a little edge."

tomboy style . . .

I, like many women, don't identify with cupcakes and flowers all the time, so it's fun to mix things up with sporty accents. I live in my boyfriend's closet—I throw on his shirts all the time! I often leave a few buttons undone, exposing a pop of color or a lacy bra top. And these gladiator wedges are strong without sacrificing sexy, casual while staying current.

. . . with femme touches

With so many manly motifs, this look needed some superwoman accessories to soften it up. The silver shoestring belt defines the waist of the chunky shorts, and this Luxirare cuff is supersleek and modern but also has a traditional tribal vibe. I topped this look off with feminine, vintage-inspired cat's-eye shades and silver rings.

I play a lot with texture—it can amp up even the most simplistic of looks. That's why I love these basic shorts in an unexpected knit! The turban is also a bit surprising—I got it for $3 at a beauty supply store, and its polyester folds make for a more structured, exotic version of the slouchy beanie.

build your look

GET A LEG UP

Jazzi McCilbort | Jazzi McG | Los Angeles, U.S.A

There's a hearty dose of contradiction in wearing booty shorts made of heavy winter knit. Since I'm a petite girl—about 5 feet (1.5 m) tall on a good day—I love to play up my legs as much as possible, so I wear a lot of high-waisted cuts that elongate my torso and hint at my love of retro fashion.

"I really like stripes combined with these chic and **timeless navy blue** shorts. I seldom dress for occasions, but this look was perfect for staying out in the rain on a **summer day."**

Aurélia Scheyé | Fashion Is a Playground | Paris, France

SKIRT BASICS

The great thing about a well-fitting skirt is that it's totally adaptable. And no matter how casually you style it, it'll always be more feminine and polished than jeans. When trying one on, check that it doesn't ride up or scoot around your hips when you walk, and that any slits open and close without incident.

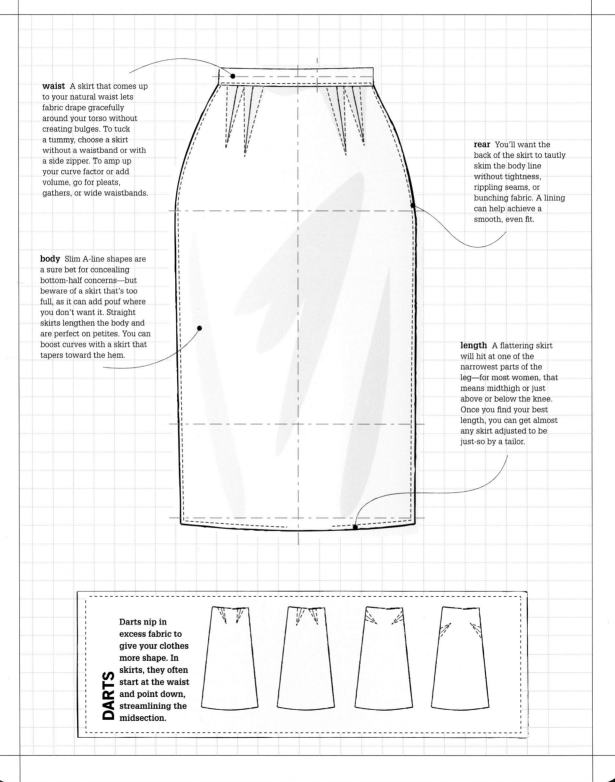

waist A skirt that comes up to your natural waist lets fabric drape gracefully around your torso without creating bulges. To tuck a tummy, choose a skirt without a waistband or with a side zipper. To amp up your curve factor or add volume, go for pleats, gathers, or wide waistbands.

body Slim A-line shapes are a sure bet for concealing bottom-half concerns—but beware of a skirt that's too full, as it can add pouf where you don't want it. Straight skirts lengthen the body and are perfect on petites. You can boost curves with a skirt that tapers toward the hem.

rear You'll want the back of the skirt to tautly skim the body line without tightness, rippling seams, or bunching fabric. A lining can help achieve a smooth, even fit.

length A flattering skirt will hit at one of the narrowest parts of the leg—for most women, that means midthigh or just above or below the knee. Once you find your best length, you can get almost any skirt adjusted to be just-so by a tailor.

DARTS Darts nip in excess fabric to give your clothes more shape. In skirts, they often start at the waist and point down, streamlining the midsection.

skirt length
There's no one right length—the secret is all in balancing the proportions. You can defrumpify a maxi skirt with a breezy cami on top, or pair a mini with a chunky sweater for a less scandalous look.

Pleat Types

Different types of pleating allow movement, affect a garment's amount of volume and how it hangs on the body, and can take the tone of your outfit from scholarly coed to playful pixie to vintage sophisticate.

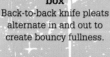

basic accordion
Narrow, evenly spaced, and permanent creases add eye-pleasing texture.

box
Back-to-back knife pleats alternate in and out to create bouncy fullness.

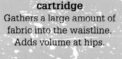

cartridge
Gathers a large amount of fabric into the waistline. Adds volume at hips.

micromini

mini

honeycomb
Narrow, rolled pleats are pressed flat, then smocked for geometric intrigue.

kick
This single pleat is added to the front or back of a narrow skirt for mobility.

knife
Accordion pleats are pressed flat to point in a single direction.

midi

plissé
Narrow pleats, usually on silk, that are set when wet for a crinkly, drapey effect.

rolled
Tubular pleats are pinched and stitched down for full shape from waist to hem.

sunburst
Accordion pleats are draped on the bias so they fall open toward the hem.

tea-length

ballerina

maxi

SKIRTS
take your pick

pencil
Skims the body and hits near the knee. Sophisticated and totally versatile.

A-line
Flares gently from the natural waist. Look for a charming knee-length hem.

rah-rah
Short knife pleats bring a cheerful or playfully subversive edge to any outfit.

flounce
A gathered piece of fabric at the hem draws attention to pretty legs.

godet
Fabric inserts sewn into the skirt create a flared shape and swingy movement.

handkerchief
Uneven layers, often of sheer or drapey fabric, create a skirt for a modern sprite.

shirt
Tied shirt arms lend the look of an oversize Oxford worn as a bottom.

bustle
Created in the late nineteenth century. Adds sexy shaping to boyish figures.

bubble
A hem drawn under and back into the waistband makes a full, bouncy shape.

Karla Deras | Karla's Closet | Simi Valley, U.S.A.

barrel
Dreamed up in early 1900s Paris. Volume at top flatters the hips and rear.

dirndl
A bell shape that's best with a sleek top. Brings the eye to a tiny waist.

circle
A skirt made from a full circle of fabric shrinks a tummy. No felt poodle required!

tulip
Petallike layers overlap in the front, creating interest on a simple shape.

tutu
Floaty tulle layers make a charming skirt that's not just for the ballet studio.

prairie
An easy, bohemian option. Try sassy shoes to avoid the frump factor.

asymmetrical
A skirt that's bias-cut and shorter on one side gives an avant-garde vibe.

corset
With a fitted, high waist and tuxedo buttons. Creates a trim middle.

mini
First liberated legs in the 1960s. Makes shorter stems look oh-so-long.

bandage
Bands of thick, stretchy material fit skintight to define and support shape.

paper bag
Gathered volume at the waist can disguise a tummy and let legs shine.

wrap
Fabric crosses over in front and ties. Be wary of sudden gusts in this skirt!

tiered
Overlapping layers strike a balance between structured and feminine.

ruffled
A wide waist and fluttery layers make curves. A sleek top keeps it modern.

balloon
A whimsical skirt with lots of volume that's drawn back in with a banded hem.

broomstick
Crinkled or knife-pleated fabric has slinky drape. Try with boots.

hobble
A narrow fit at the knees limits motion but accentuates bottom curves.

column
The long, straight shape is elegant day or night. Should just brush the floor.

SKIRT REMIX

A floor-grazing skirt is a necessity in your closet because of its chameleon abilities. This black chiffon number can be artfully draped with a lacy top and worn with sky-high heels for a romantic night out, belted as a dress and paired with a blazer for hitting downtown, or taken down a rural route with a button-down shirt, wood jewelry, and slick black boots.

Jennine Jacob | The Coveted
San Francisco, U.S.A.

a night at the opera
"I wanted to play up the sheerness of the fabric, the layers, and the silhouette, so I tucked the top layer into the waistband. I would wear this for a date night with my husband."

office glam

" As a belted strapless dress, it's classic and chic enough to be appropriate for both day and night. And for any evening engagements, all I have to do is take off the blazer! "

countryside weekend

" I've had images of Georgia O'Keeffe in my head—she was one of the most stylish women to wear long black skirts. I'm channeling the West with a chambray shirt and ankle boots. "

私はいつも

retro art

I am always inspired by art, especially Kasho Takabatake's magazine illustrations and paintings from the 1920s. They show traditional Japanese beauty and modern fashions and customs all mixed together. I also adore this vintage advertisement—the clothes are girlish, but the poster is bright and graphic and a little funny. So charming!

すてき！
オルゴールと
人形があたる
大けんしょう！！

一等賞か人形10名

、イラスト、音楽やファッションブログからインスピレーションを得ていますが、このルークの場合は自分の中にあった昔

build your look
Sailor Frills

Shan Shan | Tiny Toadstool | Osaka, Japan

I grew up at the seaside, so sailor style is always my favorite. Here, I layered a blue cotton pleated skirt over a tutu. Then I used blue, red, and white to make the look very fresh and sailor chic. A vintage wood bag with jewel ocean animals makes the whimsy complete!

mori gyaru **style**

I love the Japanese mori gyaru trend. Japanese for "forest girl," it's about layering loose, gauzy clothes and lots of girly accessories. The skirt over the tutu is hugely mori gyaru! I also used the Peter Pan collar, petals on the boating hat, and lace trim on the socks to make this look very feminine. Finally, I chose these Jeffrey Campbell clogs to toughen up the whole outfit and make it me.

Eva Lu
Huntington Beach, U.S.A.

Maria Confer | **Lulu Letty**
Court Brighton, U.S.A.

Oliwia Kijo | **Variacje**
Lodz, Poland

Lida Mankovski | **Fashionista Talk**
Santa Clara, U.S.A.

Merily Leis | **Sequin Magazine**
Saku, Estonia

girls, skirts, and bikes
CYCLING CHIC

Who says a girl can't ride a bike in a skirt?
Pick the right bike, pick the right skirt
(think A-line, with skirt guards or tights),
and show off your calves. Hey, it doesn't
hurt that drivers will notice you more.

all swept up in adventure

This outfit really reflects how I was feeling that day—young, carefree, and a little careless. To take these pictures, my boyfriend and I had to climb a giant wall on the side of a cliff. It was reckless of me—you try scaling a wall in a long skirt!—but it made me feel like I was a kid again. Also, the rugged boots ended up being incredibly practical for the climb.

fresh ideas

Spring was just around the corner when I saw these cute white flowers as I was walking by my local florist. So I bought a bouquet and simply superglued the blossoms to a black satin ribbon, then tied it into a bow around my head. I wanted to keep this look simple so the only accessories I wore were rings.

bohemian lovechild

When I wear this outfit it makes me feel like a free-spirited gypsy who wants to travel the world and live every day as it comes—I know it's a cliché but it's true! I also felt as if I had stepped straight out of Woodstock. That era, the music, the love, everyone seemed so happy without a care in the world.

build your look

Luxe Lengths

Nicole Warne | Gary Pepper Vintage | Terrigal, Australia

This is the first maxi skirt I fell in love with. It is navy blue silk, falls beautifully from the waist, and makes me feel incredibly chic. Here, I've layered it over a pink slip and worn it with boots, a floral headdress, and simple jewelry for a look that's modern and feminine. The perfectly timed wind was all Mother Nature's idea—I think it really shows the movement of the skirt and makes the entire outfit come to life!

DRESSES

DRESS BASICS

No matter the occasion, a dress with an amazing fit can make you feel undeniably special. In general, you can't go wrong with a frock that gently hugs your shape and hits at the knee. When you're trying one on, strut a bit or do a few twirls to be sure it fits just right all over.

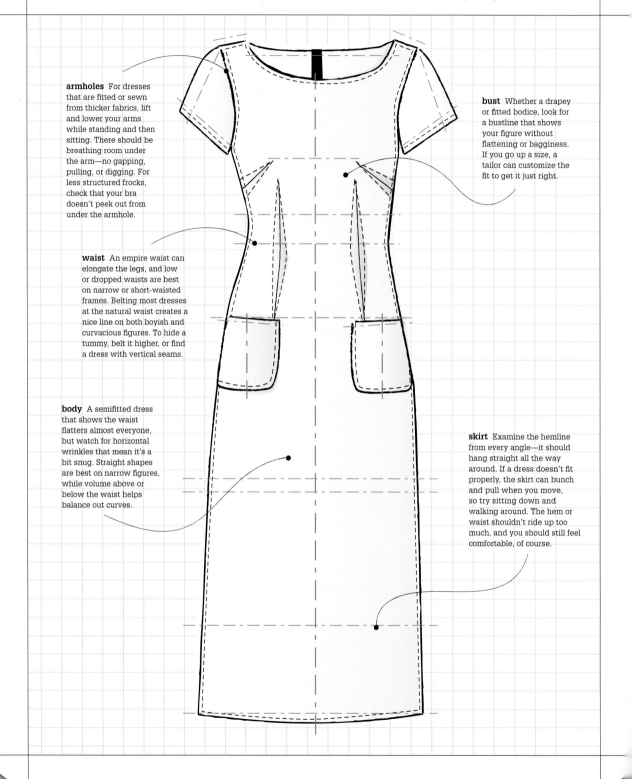

armholes For dresses that are fitted or sewn from thicker fabrics, lift and lower your arms while standing and then sitting. There should be breathing room under the arm—no gapping, pulling, or digging. For less structured frocks, check that your bra doesn't peek out from under the armhole.

bust Whether a drapey or fitted bodice, look for a bustline that shows your figure without flattening or bagginess. If you go up a size, a tailor can customize the fit to get it just right.

waist An empire waist can elongate the legs, and low or dropped waists are best on narrow or short-waisted frames. Belting most dresses at the natural waist creates a nice line on both boyish and curvaceous figures. To hide a tummy, belt it higher, or find a dress with vertical seams.

body A semifitted dress that shows the waist flatters almost everyone, but watch for horizontal wrinkles that mean it's a bit snug. Straight shapes are best on narrow figures, while volume above or below the waist helps balance out curves.

skirt Examine the hemline from every angle—it should hang straight all the way around. If a dress doesn't fit properly, the skirt can bunch and pull when you move, so try sitting down and walking around. The hem or waist shouldn't ride up too much, and you should still feel comfortable, of course.

Darts

Look for darts that begin where you need less room, and point to where you need more. For example, ladies with narrow waists and full busts will find that waist darts work wonders. If a dress's darts don't hit you in the right spots, you'll notice roomy areas that aren't filled out—and you should head to the tailor for a dart redo.

backless dresses
If you'd like to show off a beautiful back, pick a dress style with a little less coverage. Some looks are dangerously sexy; others provide just a glimpse of skin.

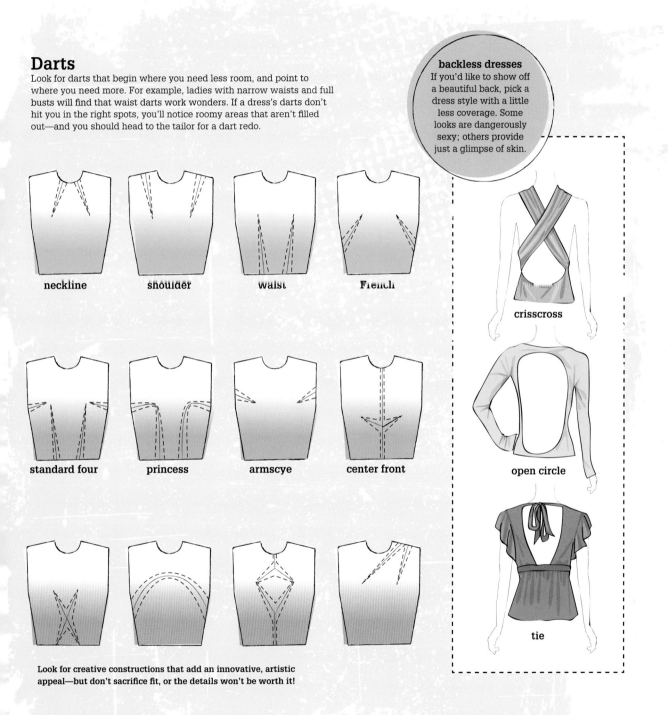

neckline

shoulder

waist

French

standard four

princess

armscye

center front

crisscross

open circle

tie

Look for creative constructions that add an innovative, artistic appeal—but don't sacrifice fit, or the details won't be worth it!

CASUAL DRESSES
take your pick

shift
A high-necked, boxy, and sleeveless dress. Perfect for everyday wear.

sheath
This curve-hugging frock debuted as an undergarment. Adds height and slims.

caftan
This breezy cloak is worn in many parts of the world. Ideal beach cover-up!

maxi
A floor-length dress. Masks fuller hips or a tummy with an empire waist.

tee shirt
This sexy, comfy classic is perfect for layering. A V-neck draws the eyes up.

shirt
A longer take on the Oxford shirt. A belt cinches the waist for feminine shape.

safari
A shirt dress on an adventure, with button tabs on the cuffs and pockets.

house
A 1950s style with a shirt-style bodice and voluminous A-line skirt.

swing
A fitted bodice with a full skirt that can really move! Pretty on large busts.

tabard
Inspired by early menswear. A boxy shape often updated by floaty fabrics.

tent
This dress hangs loose without a waistline. Go mini for a trim shape.

tunic
A basic that's perfect layered or with a belt. Look for embroidered details.

señorita
A Mexican-inspired dress that begs for tousled locks and flat sandals.

blouson
Great for balancing a top- or bottom-curvy frame. Instant waistline enhancer.

slip
A coy dress with lace details and thin straps. Flatters small bustlines.

babydoll
Supershort with an empire waist and lingerie-style straps or cap sleeves.

sundress
Especially delightful with a smocked bodice and barely there straps.

bodycon
This formfitting style shapes the figure, leaving little to the imagination.

tube
A strapless, stretchy cylinder of fabric hugs curves—if you dare to wear it!

kimono
A robe-like dress with a tie closure. Drapey sleeves offer full arm coverage.

Cristina Morales | La Petite Nymphéa
Barcelona, Spain

apron
This flirty play on the domestic apron has a slight bib in the front.

pinafore
A girlish frock that's sleeveless with a straight fit. Femmes up boyish frames.

jumper
This sleeveless, collarless dress has playful suspenders. Wear with a shirt!

combo
Gives the look of separates in a single garment for an easy, put-together look.

wrap
Highly flattering for curvy figures. Slims the waist while enhancing the bust.

sweater
A fall and winter essential that hugs for a fit that's both sexy and cozy.

coat
A shaped dress with button closure. Can be worn alone or as a top layer.

DRESS REMIX

Every woman needs a little black dress that goes anywhere, styled any way. But basic doesn't mean boring! You can create volume by gathering and pinning the skirt for an offbeat, tiered effect, or wear the dress backward and unzipped to invent an all-new neckline. If your dress has a rad detail on the torso (snarling panther print, anyone?), tuck it into a skirt and showcase the top like a tee.

Rebecca Stice | The Clothes Horse
Fort Worth, U.S.A.

DIY bubble skirt
"For a modern hem and eye-catching shape, I gathered the skirt in folds and secured my handiwork with a few safety pins. This made the skirt even shorter—leggings were a must!"

basics go backward
"Wearing this dress backward puts the zipper at center stage—plus, the panther on the back makes exiting a room pretty fun! I wore it with a vintage headband and lace-up wedges."

stealth tee
"This Tryptich dress may be a statement piece for me, but it's still flexible and versatile in my wardrobe. Here I've tucked it into a favorite thrifted leather skirt to show off the design."

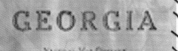

GEORGIA

NATIONAL MAP COMPANY

build your look

THE SIMPLE SUNDRESS

МѢСТО ДЛЯ МАРКИ

Rhiannon Leifheit | Liebemarlene Vintage | Atlanta, U.S.A.

This is an everyday dress for me, but it's especially good on a hot summer afternoon in Georgia, where the art of pairing light and cheerful dresses with small accessories will keep you cool. On this particular summer day, I wore it wandering around Commerce, Georgia, going to antique shops and thrift stores with my boyfriend. It's perfect because it's classic and looks great on its own, but you can make it special with tiny touches—a little goes a long way.

a nip here, a tuck there

I bought this dress on Etsy, and it was too big and very long. So one night I stayed up really late taking in the waist and hemming it—I was watching old Billy Wilder movies (like *The Apartment*) to keep me awake while I sewed! The scarf is printed with spools of thread—perfect to pair with a dress that I spent so much time sewing!

vintage vacation

When I put together this outfit, I imagined what a young American woman would wear traveling in the '40s and '50s—abroad to Nice or Monaco or just out on a drive through the countryside. Plus, at the time I was really into digging up old candid photos online and looking at the fashion in 1950s teen magazines. The dress's sweet, tiny floral print and the little kerchief around the throat are both throwbacks to that era and that on-the-road spirit.

Louise Ebel | Miss Pandora
Paris, France

Kanae Otomo | Kansairetro
Nishinomiya City, Japan

Rebecca Bergen | Fashion She Says
New York City, U.S.A.

Dyanna Pure | The SF Style
San Francisco, U.S.A.

Casey Cartwright | Elegant Musings
Brandon, U.S.A.

Eva Schon
Prague, Czech Republic

Tiffany Brandenburg | Le Blog de Sushi
Melbourne, Australia

Khrystyna Marriott | Food, Flora, and Felines
Cork, Ireland

dresses of an era
GO VINTAGE

Vintage is more than fancy talk for "heap of used clothes." A thrifted dress is a time machine to another era. Go '50s sweetheart in a lacy party dress, or '70s diva with a crochet number. Not one for costumery? Then mix a mod shift or beaded flapper with more modern items, and revel in being the only girl in "that dress" at the party.

"This dress's surprising **quilted texture** and peekaboo **crinoline** make for a great daytime-date look—**sexy but sweet.**"

Jazzi McGilbert | Jazzi McG | Los Angeles, U.S.A.

FORMAL DRESSES

take your pick

drop waist
The elongated bodice adds height to petite figures and shows off curves.

tuxedo
A sleek take on men's formalwear. Look for pintucks and a cummerbund.

ball gown
A princess-worthy style with fitted bodice and full, multilayered skirt.

goddess
Features graceful draping to create an ethereal look. Pair with strappy heels.

mermaid
Fitted through the bodice and hip, then flared from the knee for 1940s glamour.

lace overlay
Sheer lace over nude fabric. Balance the tone with less demure accessories.

empire
A flowing skirt and seam under the bust create the look of perfect proportions.

high low
A hem that's shorter in front than back draws attention to fabulous shoes.

cutaway
Sleeveless with a round, necklace-like collar. Bares nice shoulders and arms.

peplum
A gathered layer adds curve to the hips and a playful vibe to a look.

slit
Sexily shows off a toned physique. Best with bare legs and sky-high heels.

two piece
A matching bodice and skirt make a fluid look and still define the waist.

sheer panel
A fitted dress with a sweetheart neckline and mesh yoke, back, and sleeves.

split skirt
A slit reveals a different layer for a splash of color or textural interest.

Watteau
An attached cape-like piece cascades from the upper back.

princess
Two vertical seams glide from bust to hem to elongate and smooth the figure.

wiggle
Knee-length and curve-hugging, this '50s classic is a sexy take on office wear.

Basque waist
The slightly dropped, seamed waist adds curves to straighter figures.

cross neck
Twisting and draping lend softness and dimension.

wing bust
A bit of fabric folds over the décolletage to give a sexy peek of the dress's lining.

strapless
A flared style focuses attention up to the face, neck, and shoulders.

flapper
A straight shape with dropped waist and fringe that shimmies with you.

tulip
Volume at the hips creates an hourglass shape and slims the frame.

tiered
A sculptural, layered dress. A minidress version avoids a heavy look.

bustier
A must-have for small busts. Add a blazer and pumps for a hyperchic look.

party
The short, flared shape is flirty but modest enough for an upscale event.

cheongsam
A fitted dress often in satin with a mandarin collar and slits on both sides.

Sandra Hagelstam | 5 Inch and Up | London, U.K.

build your look
FLORENTINE
FINERY

Jane Aldridge | Sea of Shoes
Dallas, U.S.A.

special extras

The pink sequined belt is also D&G and I stole it from my mom when I was about twelve. I took it everywhere—I wore it with long flannel patchwork skirts in Tokyo and with Mexican tunics in San Miguel de Allende . . . I had to search high and low to get my hands on these shoes but I'm so glad that I did. When I was getting ready for the party, I couldn't make up my mind what to wear and I tried on everything I brought. I'm glad I went with this really dressy look—I rarely have an occasion to dress up like this back in Texas! Though honestly I dress up all the time, just because I like to—why not?

I had been invited to luxury retailer Luisa Via Roma's 10th anniversary party in Florence, and this is what I ended up wearing to the party. The dress is Dries van Noten from Spring 2008—I got it for a steal a year later at an outlet in Dallas. I think this look is fun and playful—the Dolce & Gabbana "face" shoes definitely show that fashion can have a sense of humor, and to me the dress's open back with beaded knot detailing is superfeminine.

style as curation

I live in suburban Texas, and it's a bit of a bubble, far away from the fashion world or cultural meccas like Florence! But Texas creates lots of eccentric artists, and I find art made by nonprofessionals really inspiring. So I get a thrill from hunting down curious creations (like these harlequin bookends) and other crafts, or creating my own fun but crude art—as evidenced by the drawings above. But for me, styling is an art—it's about creating a vision. That's what I try to do, to curate pieces I love and display them in a way that shows my respect for them.

passion for fashion

I definitely had Anna Dello Russo's playful and outrageous approach to fashion in mind when I created this look. I love her magpie eye for jewelry and glitz, and that she wears the most opulent runway looks to the fashion shows. Her sense of style is all about having fun and not being afraid to go over-the-top.

GOWN REMIX

Everyone's got one: a formal dress from a wedding or prom hanging in the back of the closet, never to be worn again. But have you tried layering it, shortening it, adding pants, or even another skirt? Dig deep in your wardrobe and consider surprising combinations that get you the most bang for your bridesmaid buck.

ladylike length
For a "meet-the-parents" hem, fold the extra fabric and cover with a shimmery belt.

look-at-me layers
Accentuate curves and create drape with a body-con dress on top. Sassy señorita!

sneaky tunic
Gather and pin the skirt at the waist, then shimmy into skinny jeans and steep booties.

formal gown

So it's not your favorite dress. Or it is, but chances for wearing it are slim. Focus on the things you do like (its ornate beading, floor-grazing train, or lovely draping) and dream up looks that put this element on display. If all else fails, get creative with your tailor.

retro wrap
Channel Betty Boop by adding a shorter wrap dress over and a fun printed belt.

instant petticoat
Make use of volume! Pin up the skirt and top with a short skirt for a punky-pouf look.

country corsetry
Head to the country by throwing on a casual bustier with a denim jacket and boots.

moody nudes

I am really into subtle brown, black, and nude combinations. If mixing brown and black is against the rules, then this fawn belt and nude shoes make the perfect partners in crime. Many of the palettes I wear are inspired by impressionist painters—I love their soft pastels and textured brushstrokes—but I'm also inspired by the delectable colors of candy and cupcakes.

Seventies Vixen

Liz Cherkasova | Late Afternoon | San Francisco, U.S.A.

For me, fashion is just the adult version of a childhood game of dress-up. My wardrobe has inklings of '70s mystique (like crochet dresses and fringe), but it's updated with deep jewel tones and effortless draping. I wanted to exude sexy, glamorous energy for a romantic night out, so I built this look around a vintage lace-overlay dress and added a faux-fur collar and loads of silver jewelry to glam it up.

from Moscow with love

This clutch is very special to me—it was given to me by my grandmother, who still lives in Moscow. Every time I carry it I am reminded of her and how careful and thoughtful she was to preserve such a delicate bag! I'm inspired by my Russian heritage—these nesting babushka dolls feature a swirling, lacy pattern, just like my dress and clutch. In Russian, *babushka* means "grandmother," and every babushka is painted a little differently, so each one is unique.

COLORS
& FABRICS

COLOR BASICS

So what colors look good on you?

Your best colors are those that make you look just great—that make your skin appear fresh, your eyes vivid, your smile bright, and your hair lustrous and rich in tone.

To discover these shades, hold up a white piece of paper to your face—does your cheek look rosy or slightly blue? If so, then your skin has cool undertones. If your cheek looks more yellow or orange, then your skin's undertones are warm. In general, you'll want to try and wear colors that match and enhance your skin's natural undertones.

If there's lots of contrast between your skin, eyes, and hair, then your color type is considered clear, and you'll look best in clothes and makeup that play up this contrast. If the difference between your features is less defined, then your color type is considered muted and you'll be flattered by softer, nuanced shades that don't overpower.

Here, you'll find shades that look great on specific skin types. But the best way to tell is to hold up garments to your face in colors that you like and see if they flatter you. Sometimes the most flattering colors aren't the ones you like the best, but don't rule them out: You can always find ways to sneak them into your outfits and still look great.

camel
Intensely contrasting, warm skin types look even bolder next to a rich, warm neutral.

bright orange
To rock a top in a color outside your ideal palette, use a scarf or necklace in a flattering hue to make your face look bright.

salmon pink
Sunny pastels do a lot for warm, clear coloring, especially for skin undertones with a peach tint.

true red
Intense, bright hues (like fire-engine red) flatter cool undertones and clear, high-contrast skin, hair, and eye color combos.

burgundy
A deeper red with a little more purple is better for women who have warm skin tones and high-contrast eyes and hair.

golden yellow
Opt for a bold yellow to suit high-contrast, warm undertones and to enhance light eye color.

bright gold
Make warm skin tones really glow by adding a gold statement necklace next to your face.

neon yellow
Try more difficult colors in accessories that are far away from your face—like bright neon leggings.

moss green
Lend a little contrast to warm skin tones and muted eye and hair colors with a top in an earthy tone.

emerald green
Deep greens with a bit of blue pick up natural sparkle in the eyes of those with both cool or warm complexions.

icy blue
Chilly pastels will flatter clear, cold skin tones—and make pale eyes really pop.

bright aqua
A bright aqua will intensify muted gray or blue eyes and electrify warm skin and hair.

lavender
Muted, warm features benefit from other soft shades—try a lovely lavender.

soft denim
Wear a soft denim top to play up muted features that have warm undertones.

navy
Navy's a go-to neutral for women with high-contrast, cool-colored features.

eggplant
This shade's blend of red and blue complements both warm and cool complexions.

cobalt
If a beloved color is too bold for your skin, but works with colors in your palette, try it in a small dose, like a bag.

COMPLEMENTARY COLORS

take your pick

Want your outfit to pop with high-contrast color? Try complementary shades, which are opposite on the color wheel and make each other appear brighter when combined.

Ilanka Verhoeven | Fashionnerdic
Rotterdam, Netherlands

orange and blue
This is an all-out attention-grabber. Try it in small, isolated doses, like a blue bag with an orange dress.

yellow and purple
Darker shades create a near regal look. Go for softer tints like lemon and violet for a sweeter vibe.

red and green
Opt for tones like maroon and olive (reds and greens with gray in them) to avoid a holiday theme.

muted
Tone it down with lighter tints, or opt for a contrasting accessory as a more subtle accent color.

bright
When rocking separates that boldly contrast, wear the bright item where you want to draw the eye's focus.

ANALOGOUS COLORS
take your pick

Wearing colors that are side by side on the color wheel makes for a harmonious, nuanced look. This scheme is softer than a complementary combo, and more dynamic than a single-color look.

warm pairings
Be zesty with yellows and oranges. Pick one as the main color, then add bright touches of another.

cool pairings
Mutliple blue hues result in a peaceful, pleasing look that's often found in nature. Think blue sky over water.

Susie Lau | Style Bubble | London, U.K.

pattern explosion
Mixing patterns can be tricky. Go for prints in analogous colors for an eclectic yet inarguably polished look.

MONO CHROMATIC REMIX

Hit one note and hit it good with a one-color look from head to toe. Dressing all in one color makes you look long and lean, and it's a great way to translate your mood into an outfit that lets everyone know how you're feeling. Go sunbeam yellow for a playful state of mind, reflecting-pond blue for a zen-chic feel, or tone-on-tone brown for a sophisticated look that'll make black jealous. To avoid a washed-out effect, try separates in slightly different hues, and add lots of texture for visual variety.

Zanita Whittington
Sydney, Australia

silly in citrus
"This look was inspired by bananas and lemons, two very fabulous fruits. It was worn as a joke (the crown is from a Christmas bon-bon!), but I'd wear it to the park on a sunny day."

Michelle Koesnadi | Glisters & Blisters
Jakarta, Indonesia

true blue
"I wanted to emphasize one color to make a normal jeans-'n'-tank combo look more polished. This look is minimalist, but it still stands out in a crowd. Plus, blue makes me feel calm!"

Justyna Baraniecki | Chichichichic!
Ottawa, Canada

chocolate glamour
"I like drama in my clothes! Basics with a little glam make the everyday ennui easier to bear. In this outfit I went to the post office, then took the dog on a walk. You live once—dress like it!"

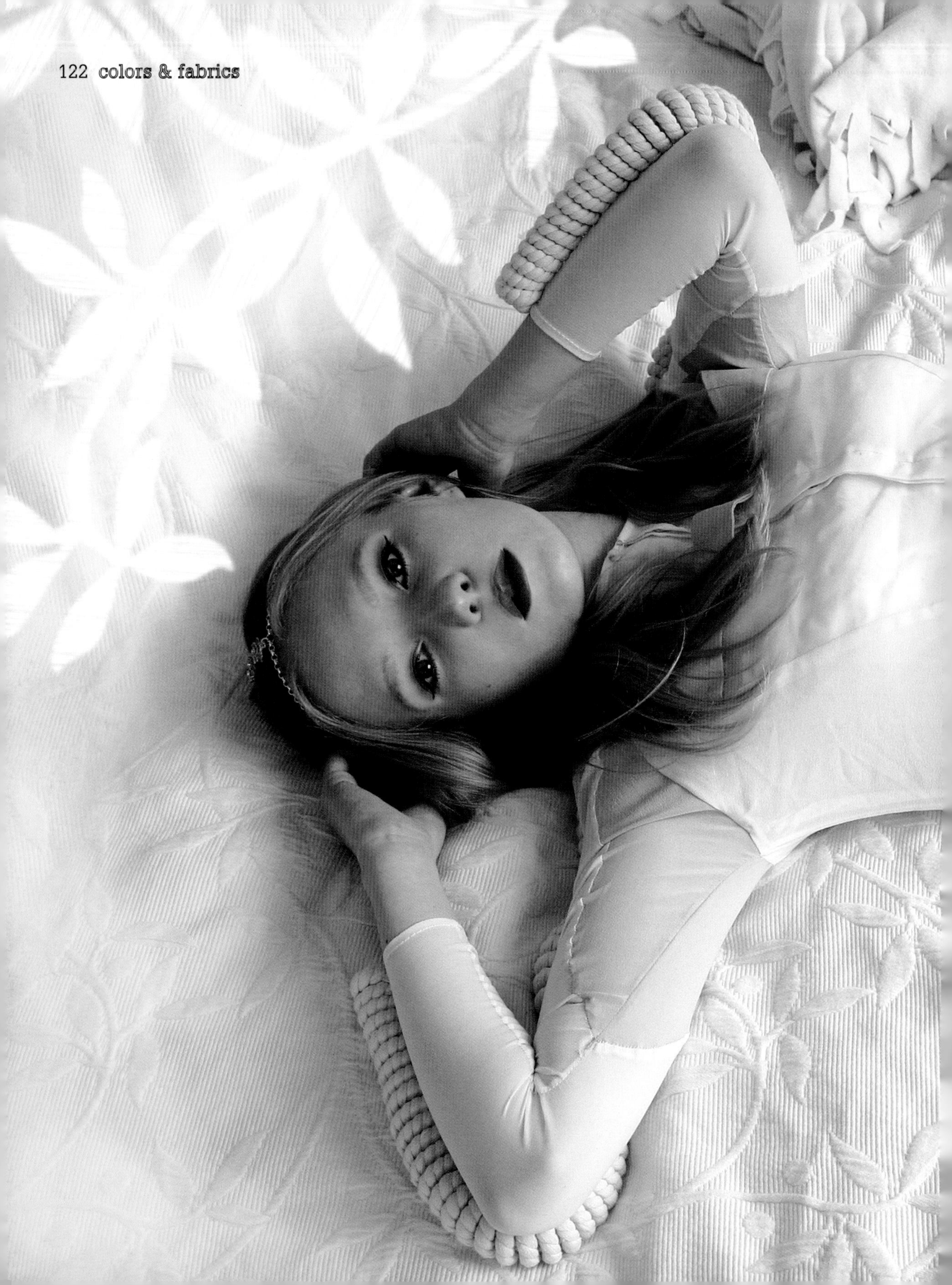

"I like giving simple, **monochromatic** looks a **twist** with bright **red lipstick!**"

Carolina Engman | Fashion Squad | Stockholm, Sweden

**class-act
accent**

In the name of classing it up, I've come close to forsaking my trusted color. But wearing little flashes of it is just right—its boldness creates contrast. I think that red and black, while a great combo, sometimes can be a bit harsh, so I integrated the gray to soften up the severity of the color palette. It also helps to have interesting textures so that the color doesn't steal the show—the lace skirt goes a long way!

build your look

RUBY FLASH

Jennine Jacob | The Coveted | New York City, U.S.A.

If I weren't a color slut, I'd declare red my favorite color. Red has always lured me with its sultry ways—I probably have enough red clothes to wear complete head-to-toe red all week. Here, I use it as an accent color, letting it peek out from layers of black and gray.

look to the skyline

I'm really affected by architecture. In Chicago, where I was living when I wore this look, there's a lot of concrete, brick, and iron black—Chicago has a very old industrial downtown. Looking back, I can see that this outfit has a lot of those deep colors and structural details—lots of square shapes and gritty textures.

fashion improv

I made these legwarmers out of a sweater from the Frankfurt Flea Market. I was really broke and living in Germany, and had to make Christmas presents for everyone, but I kept the legwarmers for myself. The wool cardigan is also from the flea market—it was at the 2 euro table instead of the 1 euro table, and boy have I gotten my 2 euros' worth! I've mixed these thrifted items with a Jean-Paul Gaultier silk cutout tunic, a red Marc Jacobs cuff, and Stuart Weitzman shoes.

Carrie Harwood | Wish Wish Wish
London, U.K.

Susie Lau | Style Bubble
London, U.K.

Anna Bu | Bu The Right Thing
Hanover, Germany

Tavi Gevinson | Style Rookie
Oak Park, U.S.A.

Arushi Khosla | Fab Blab
Delhi, India

Jane Aldridge | Sea of Shoes
Dallas, U.S.A.

the bright stuff
NEON

Rock down to electric avenue with brazen, daring, over-the-top fluorescents. You can get a modest jolt from a small piece, like a braided headband, pumps, or quirky DIY pom-pom embellishments. Or you can make others blink by wearing dazzling, all-over color: Try day-glo leggings, an oversize tie-dye shirt, or a fuzzy psychedelic coat.

balance the brights
I love playing with colors that are next to analogous—in this case, pink, orange, and yellow. I paired these vivid colors with soft neutrals in gray and brown. (The last thing I wanted to do was drown them with fail-safe black!) Flecks of turquoise in the necklace and belt make the whole look come together.

fit for a picnic

I'm very romantic when it comes to my wardrobe—the pieces I buy must fill my head with fantasies of what could happen when I wear them. This dress's colors make me dream of sitting on a dock and enjoying fresh raspberries and lemonade.

build your look

TROPICS IN WINTER

Rebecca Stice | The Clothes Horse | Fort Monroe, U.S.A.

I envisioned wearing this dress during warmer months, but it arrived on a drizzly and miserable January afternoon—so I immediately threw it on to bring some summer color into my day. Then I started adding heavier pieces that would help me weather the temperature outside—all without sacrificing my summer sartorial fantasy.

by the seaside

My style icons are stars from classic films (like Gidget and Clara Bow) and women in vintage ads, like this one that hangs in my room. I love the bathing beauty in the poster, and the parasol's punchy hues spoke to my dress's colors. I added spectator booties to further channel the advertisement's retro feel.

aloha au iaoe

I lived in Hawaii and loved its explosion of color—the vivid blue of the sky and the bright orange of hibiscus. The people there are the happiest I've ever met—I think that's why Hawaii's colors can always transform my mood.

seersucker

A jaunty gently puckered fabric that's lightweight and usually features pastel stripes.

raw silk

Not heavily processed, this fabric is covered with naturally nubby "nolls" for beautiful texture.

poplin

The most ubiquitous of shirt fabrics, poplin is light, crisp, and versatile, with a smooth finish.

watercolor

Fabric that's been dripped or splattered with colorful dye is wistful, vibrant, and vaguely floral.

swiss dot

A romantic raised dot pattern created by weaving the dots, then tufting them off so they stand out.

patent leather

Flats or a belt in shiny-finished leather can push your outfit into the realm of glossy, ladylike chic.

lace

Channel the vibe of a Victorian lawn party, but make it modern by pairing lace with faded denim or boots.

Jazzi McGilbert | Jazzi McG
Los Angeles, U.S.A.

chambray

A cotton material resembling lightweight denim, this casual fabric has a slight rough-and-tumble edge.

cotton twill

Sturdy and diagonally woven, this fabric is dressier than jeans while staying breathable and versatile.

eyelet

A sweet pattern of cutouts and embroidery. Can be all over or placed on a sleeve, neckline, or hem.

cotton pique

A light and stretchy knit with a raised, woven design most often found on polo shirts.

garden floral

A fabric scattered with oversize blossoms captures the season's spirit. Try in a '50s-style dress.

liberty floral

A tiny, allover floral print, this delicate signature of 1930s fashion was trendy in the '60s and the '90s.

silk chiffon

A superthin, sheer, and floaty fabric that creates ethereal dresses, blouses, and lingerie.

SPRING FABRICS

take your pick

Strip off wintertime's layers and jump out into the enchantingly fresh world of spring; it's the season for playing with hyperfeminine and charmingly polished fabrics and silhouettes. If sweet and proper isn't quite your thing, try balancing out a liberty-floral dress with combat boots, or layering a patent-leather belt over ripped jeans.

POLKA DOT REMIX

Get your dot on with a print that goes classic-sweet or full-on modern. A tiny dose on tights adds a dash of school-girl charm, while a black polka-dot skirt over a pastel dress can stave off sugar overload. For smart texture, mix and match dots with circular studs.

Mayo Wo | Fleas on Glam Robe
Hong Kong, China

sweet spots
"I feel younger in this outfit, like I've been transported back to my childhood. And the dress's nude chiffon makes me feel dreamy. This is perfect for a walk in the woods."

dots upon dots
"This is something I'd wear for my daily routine. I love the contrast between the toughness of studs and the girliness of polka dots, plus the pale pink color of my ankle boots."

sharpen up pastels
"This look is modern romantic—the colors are sweet, like macarons. You can't see here, but the thigh-highs have hearts up the back. It'd be nice to go on a lunch date in this look."

build your look

Self-Portrait in Spring

Chantal Van Der Meijden | Cocorosa | New York City, U.S.A.

I love spring fabrics, like dusty, muted silks and chiffons. I think it's because a cherry blossom tree bloomed in my front yard when I was growing up in the Netherlands, and I've loved airy, gauzy spring textures and colors ever since! This look's silk dress also reminds me of old English porcelain. Its drapery, palette, and bow all create such a wistful sensibility—I feel like I am channeling porcelain's sweetness with this outfit.

ikat

Originating in Malaysia, this fabric's yarns are dyed before weaving, resulting in a special blurred effect.

Pucci-inspired

A vibrant, swooshing pattern in kaleidoscope colors. First hit the scene with fashionistas in the '50s.

burnout jersey

A jersey's surface is unevenly worn for sexy hints of transparency. Tones down more structured pieces.

linen

Nothing's kinder in the heat than natural, breathable linen made from flax. Watch out for easy wrinkling.

gingham

A wholesome and cheerful two-color woven check pattern that's pitch-perfect for a summertime picnic.

batik

An African method of wax-resist dyeing uses natural colors and makes layered, exotic patterns.

mesh

A netlike, breathable fabric that's a mix of sporty and '80s glam. Layer it over contrasting hues for dimension.

geometric

Stop traffic in a bold, graphic pattern made up of artistic angles. Simple, yet sophisticated and playful.

madras

Lightweight cotton plaids are often printed or sewn in a patchwork for breezy, beach-ready looks.

nostalgia for the exotic

I love to go to rich, cultural places for inspiration,
especially lush antique fabrics. This kimono is from
Topshop, but it feels as if it is from another time and place.
It is shimmery and sheer but ladylike, and it makes me daydream
of a faraway bedroom. I am also drawn to Baroque embellishments
because I love the lavish layers and drapery you see in marble sculptures.

rough-and-tumble romantic

To edge out simple pastel colors I
always turn to boots. These black
studded foldover ones stop the look
from going overboard on
sweetness. For a casual and
offhand feel, I cut off regular
leggings to make them into slouchy
footless knee-high socks. The silk
dress is hoisted up with a skinny
gold vintage belt—it gives the
dress volume and body and makes
it look a little careless and rumpled,
but in a very good way!

fierce fashion icon

This look was inspired by 1980s pop icon Grace Jones, a Jamaica-born star famous for her defiant but elegant style—she definitely marches to her own beat and defines her own trends. Her look is flamboyant, with sharp shapes and menswear-inspired padding. Hence this outfit has a touch of androgyny, but it still favors the feminine side. My hairstyle here is an homage to her!

SAY IT LOUD

Funeka Ngwevela | The Quirky Stylista | Johannesburg, South Africa

This matching top and leggings set is brave and bold, two things I strive to be every day. I love playing with larger-than-life prints. This one reminds me of rebirth—its bright, oversize flowers make me think of summer, so we shot in a landscape that captured that essence. Putting this retro look together wasn't by chance, but finding the perfect goats to costar? That took a little luck!

back to my roots

Regular ingredients of my looks are nonconformity, female empowerment, and tough sophistication. I'm inspired by Camagwini, a local jazz singer and a dear friend. Her voice and style are all rooted deep in African soil; her spiritual connection with our ancestors is indescribable and immensely admirable.

DJ style

I could see myself in an early '90s hip-hop band when I put all these bright pieces together—playing with Will Smith or DJ Jazzy Jeff. The soft, scuffed shoes are perfect for break-dancing, and give the whole look a casual feel. The red sunglasses and lipstick pick up on the outfit's bright colors and make the color scheme more deliberate.

cotton gauze
Loosely woven, delicate fibers often have a deliberately crinkled look. No need to worry about wrinkles.

chevron
A multicolored pattern of converging Vs on a loose, textural knit that drapes flatteringly.

nautical stripes
Contrasting horizontal stripes add a charming, French-inspired feel. Easy to pair with other patterns.

crochet
A handmade, open knit with a lacy appearance for old-world daintiness. Try as a top layer or accessory.

tie-dye
Fabric is twisted or folded, then dyed for a pattern that's straight out of the summer of love.

silk ombré
Vibrant colors fade into a dip-dyed gradient, making a dramatic impact on a flowing dress or tunic.

lamé
Summer is not the time for subtlety. Rock some metallics for a look that's as hot as the weather.

SUMMER FABRICS

take your pick

Feeling polished under the summer sun's heat can seem impossible. But work with the weather! Combine lightweight or openwork fabrics with ones that pack a serious punch of color or a metallic splash, and you'll keep your confidence—and cool—while your outfit radiates as intensely as the sidewalk.

"I found this dress in a **flea market** some years ago and thought it would be perfect for walking in the park during a beautiful **summer sunset.** Sometimes it's the **simplest things** that make us happiest!"

Cristina Morales | La Petite Nymphéa | Barcelona, Spain

high-contrast fashion
STRIPES

No matter what era, stripes have always had a crisp, classic look. Keep it elegant with an all-over pattern, or pick small accessories in bold black-and-white bands. Whether balanced with solids or color-coordinated with subtle prints, stripes (even horizontal ones!) can be more figure-flattering than you might think.

Iris Gravemaker | Fashion Zen
Middelburg, Netherlands

Clara Campelo | Zebratrash
Rio Branco, Brazil

Cristina Morales | La Petite Nymphéa
Barcelona, Spain

Barbara Zanella | Nao Sou Sua Playmobil
Santa Catarina, Brazil

Coco Mayaki
Krakow, Poland

Yuki Lo | Oriental Sunday
Shanghai, China

Chantal Van Der Meijden | Cocorosa
New York City, U.S.A.

animal print
From leopard to zebra, these prints don't have to be on real skins to exude swanky luxury.

felt
Wool is crafted into a thick, dense material that gives garments like jackets a warm, folksy feel.

crocodile leather
Exotic, richly textured animal skins add an edgy contrast to traditional fall patterns and neutrals.

toile
This old-school French export features pastoral scenes, usually printed in just two colors.

pointelle
A ribbed knit with systematically dropped stitches. Charming on everything from tights to cardis.

tartan
A Scottish pattern of crisscrossing colors. Whether on a skirt or scarf, it's a perennial autumn favorite.

suede
Made from the underside of a hide. A little more raw than smooth leathers, with a softer nap.

Shannon Licari | Dirty Hair Halo
Minneapolis, U.S.A.

flannel

Whether solid or with a '90s-grunge plaid pattern, flannel has soft drape and a slightly fuzzy hand.

thermal

A knitting technique creates tiny pockets that trap warmth and add pretty, subtle texture.

marled knit

Multiple colors of yarn are knit together to form a garment with lots of texture and dimension.

paisley

The swirling pattern of droplet shapes originated in India. Lush and regal, it can also be psychedelic.

corduroy

Ridges, or "wales," and a velvety texture lend a laid-back, professorial vibe and pair well with patterns.

cashmere

Gathered from goats, it's the softest, finest wool. Look for investment sweaters that you'll love for years.

argyle

A knit diamond pattern that's classically chic. Contrast it with shredded denim or studded leather.

FALL FABRICS

take your pick

When brisk weather hits and makes you crave a little opulence, go for distinctive fabrics that you can layer into sleek though warm ensembles. Pair a suede skirt with a paisley blouse or an animal-print shell with a marled knit, and you'll feel rich and sumptuous during this limbo-like season.

decadent menswear

I find men's pieces to produce the most delightful and unexpected forms on a woman's body—resulting in something often quite feminine. I found the fluidity of these faux-leather trousers played nicely with the sweater's all-engulfing, slouchy shape. The bag was originally a document holder, but it works great as a huge clutch, and this velvet hat was my first-ever fedora, the one that prompted my hat obsession. The strappy heels were a last-minute addition to spruce up an otherwise relaxed look, and the gold locket lends a bit of sparkle.

channeling the marchesa

I was on a mission to find the perfect faux-fur stole when eBay threw up this beauty—I love drowning myself in it. It echoes my fondness for Luisa Casati, an Italian marchesa who embodied the grandiose eccentricity of early twentieth-century Europe and inspired artists like Man Ray. She was famous for wearing live snakes as jewelry and taking nightly strolls accompanied by cheetahs on diamond leashes, all while naked under her luxurious furs. You'd go to dinner at her house, and there would be lavishly dressed mannequins seated right next to you at the table.

build your look

Penchant for Paisley

Nadia Sarwar | Frou Frouu | London, U.K.

What initially drew me to this vintage sweater
was its paisley print in beautifully muted tones.
The design is printed rather than woven, and
looks somewhat coarse up close. My love of
paisley actually stems from childhood memories
of bits and pieces around the house—my father's
silk dressing gown, whimsical clothes made for
me by my mother, and odd cushions on sofas.

Marcella Lau | Fashion Distraction
Auckland, New Zealand

Jane Aldridge | Sea of Shoes
Dallas, U.S.A.

Marianne Theodorsen | Styledevil
Oslo, Norway

Aurélia Scheye | Fashion Is a Playground
Paris, France

Marla Singer | Versicle
Yogyakarta, Indonesia

Meijia Shao
Shanghai, China

Cilen Kurt | Cleo in Love
Istanbul, Turkey

Dar Mashiah | Fashion Pea
Haifa, Israel

Clara Campelo | Zebratrash
Rio Branco, Brazil

an enduring trend
ANIMAL PRINT

Wearing a bold pelt-inspired print can coax an appreciative purr from anyone on the street. The trick is in taming that pattern for an effect that says safari chic, not accident at the zoo. Start with small doses (scarves, shoes, headbands, or clutches), then wear it large and in charge with a furry jacket or sweeping caftan. No matter what your spirit animal, every fashionista should try styling on the wild side.

Charlene O'Rourke | s.t.r.u.t.t.
London, U.K.

houndstooth
This broken-check pattern of two colors is an old-school but still lively choice for suiting and accessories.

bouclé
Woven from multiple strands of varying tautness. The looser threads form a loopy, plush surface.

leather
From boots to blazers, its supple texture is the pinnacle of sexy luxe and gets even better as it wears in.

fur
An unmistakable symbol of luxury and refinement. Buying vintage—or faux!—fur doesn't harm animals.

herringbone
A V-shaped weave made from two shades. Named for its resemblance to a herring fish's skeleton.

chenille
Lofty, soft, and iridescent, this fabric made from twisted yarn is equally ideal for a sweater or scarf.

tweed
Heavyweight fabric woven from several colors of yarn. Won't absorb mioisture on damp winter days.

Fair Isle
A knitting technique that uses colorful yarn to produce vibrant and whimsical geometric patterns.

chunky knit
Knits with loose weave or thick, heavy yarn have a handmade look and nostalgic appeal.

shearling

A sheep or lamb hide—leather on one side and shorn on the other—is rustic-chic as a boot or coat lining.

velvet

Tufted threads are cut for a dense, soft pile. Wear in deep colors to add a regal feel to any outfit.

merino wool

Merino sheep produce wool that's incredibly soft and toasty-warm yet breathable. Perfect for layering.

brocade

Heavy fabric with a raised pattern and often a subtle sheen. Stunning for formal dresses and jackets.

satin

Usually made from silk, satin has exquisite luster and drape—just the thing for winter evening wear.

cable knit

Cotton or wool is crafted into thick fabric with a raised rope-like pattern for preppy, cozy sweaters.

buffalo plaid

A broad check, often red and black or white and black. Pair with boots and a scarf to get campfire-ready.

WINTER FABRICS

take your pick

You'll be wearing lots of layers whether you want to or not—so embrace them! Wintertime is right for exploring combinations of texture. Go decadent with a velvet coat, fur collar, and leather clutch. Or juxtapose functional fabrics with luxurious ones—a cozy buffalo-plaid jacket over a fitted satin or brocade dress might just be the best of both worlds.

build your look

DRESSED FOR A WINTER WONDERLAND

Barbro Andersen | Oslo, Norway

I love crashing different textures and fabrics into each other, particularly leather and knit. A leather dress makes such a strong statement by itself, but with a chunky knit it looks softer and more interesting. I added a cotton shirt, sheer tights, a perforated leather belt, and leather heels to lift it all to the next level.

frosty fashion
I grew up in northern Norway, where fjords and beaches are a great contrast to mountains and glaciers—I'm always very inspired by the rawness of these settings. I recently moved farther south to Oslo, and this look is kind of like small-town girl meets city-chic woman: vintage vs. high-fashion and knits vs. leather.

biker style

My mom and dad have always been enthusiastic about motorcycles. I remember seeing their leather jackets during my childhood, and I know I wasn't even a year old the first time I sat on one of those speed machines! I'm sure growing up around bikes has helped shape my love of leather in all colors and styles.

FAIR ISLE REMIX

When the winter winds blow, cut the chill with a folksy Fair Isle knit. Whether as hosiery in a multipattern mash-up, a bold head-to-toe print broken up by a belted scarf, or a quiet motif on a subtle sweater, this frost-ready fabric does triple duty: cozy, cute, and endlessly stylable.

Lini Trinh | Schanh Diu Fashion
Hanover, Germany

pattern-tastic
"These blue and white knee socks have a print like my sweater's, so I paired them with blue dotted shorts to be fun and cheeky. And I added ear muffs—I collect them, they're so cute!"

Sania Claus
Stockholm, Sweden

Helene Ryden
Nässjö, Sweden

modernist meets bohemian
"I don't believe one needs a reason to wear a special outfit. I can see myself dancing around yellow, red, and brown leaves in this sweater set. I'd love to wear it during fall in Central Park."

Scandinavian retro
"I wore this Lusekofta sweater on the first day that was cold enough for it! I added a matching mustard hat and beige tights—for me, this look captures the feeling of Scandinavian thrifting."

"We had a **beautiful sunset** and I snapped some pictures in front of the **pillow fort** I'd made. This warm lamb vest and lacy bed coat went just great with the **cozy shambles.**"

Jane Aldridge | Sea of Shoes | Dallas, U.S.A.

SHOES

FLATS
take your pick

ballet
A simple, graceful pair with a slim sole. Often has a string tie at the toe.

bow
Contrast the ultrafeminine vibe with tailored or punky pieces.

buckle
A metal detail gives a polished, professional touch to a ladylike shape.

Oxford
This basic men's shoe is refined and playfully bold in a woman's wardrobe.

brogue
Originally a countryside shoe, with perforation along the seams.

loafer
Tuck a penny in front, or choose a tasseled version. Suave and spirited.

jazz
An Oxford-style shoe with softer construction that flexes with the foot.

chukka
An ankle-high boot often in leather or canvas with two to three eyelet pairs.

slip-on
Low profile and laceless. A take on the sneaker with a slacker vibe.

espadrille slip-on
Sturdy canvas sits atop a rope sole for a sleek, breezy shoe with rustic appeal.

canvas skimmer
Try this cross between a sneaker and a ballet flat for easygoing chic.

tabi
A Japanese style that separates the big toe and has a thin, flexible sole.

cork sole
Wear with a modern or edgy ensemble to avoid going over-the-top treehugger.

flip-flop
A Y-shaped strap goes between the toes for a barely there look and feel.

thong sandal
A strip passes between toes but leaves you practically barefoot.

toe-ring sandal
A strap around the big toe makes a more structured version of a flip-flop.

embellished
A little glitz perks up a basic outfit or adds whimsy to a dressy one.

ankle strap
Showcases the foot much like a sandal, but with a modest, cute closed toe.

skimmer
Pair simple flats with tights or pants in the same color for a lean line.

pointed skimmer
The pointed toe elongates legs and makes a basic shoe more elegant.

Mary Jane
The crossover strap evokes girlhood. For a classic look, go for black patent leather.

China flat
A Mary Jane made of soft, pliable canvas that's girly but a little grungy.

monk
Double straps cross over and buckle as an alternative to boring old laces.

saddle
A dapper, two-toned style most often found in traditional black and white.

boat
Preppy and classic American styling. A special sole won't slip on wet surfaces.

moccasin
A leather or suede slip-on with a stitched toe and often fringed detail.

side tie
This mix of moccasin and Oxford is funky but elegant.

Wallabee
A thick crepe sole and moccasin-style toe box is comfy and walkable.

skate
A bit of padding helps these kicks hold up to bumps and grinds.

adhesive
Crossover hook-and-loop strips make a grown-up version of a kid's shoe.

low-top
First created for basketball; loved for its counterculture-chic history.

high-top
Folded down or laced all the way up, they'll always look street smart.

hip-hop
Look for crazy colors, stripes, and padding, or eye-catching patterns.

trainer
Engineered for support and comfort. A foolproof weekend choice.

huarache
Woven leather on a thin sole gives a wordly twist to a summer staple.

wrap
Crisscrossing ribbon or leather straps wind sexily around the ankle and calf.

ankle-cuff
The slouchy ankle piece makes it part gladiator sandal, part ankle bootie.

strappy
An ankle strap can make the legs look shorter, so it's best with a slight lift.

asymmetrical
An unexpected strap construction draws the eye to dainty ankles.

jelly
A quirky shoe of woven, clear plastic that's often glittery or brightly colored.

fancy trimming
Find some flirty trim, then use fabric glue or stitching to add frills to the edge.

preppy stripes
Get a little extra credit by gluing or sewing on multicolored ribbons and cute buttons.

all chained up
Pierce a small hole in the shoe's back, loop a jump ring through it, and attach fun chains.

FLAT REMIX

Functionality and flats go hand in hand . . . or foot in shoe. But flats can be just as stylish as stilettos, especially when you experiment! Choose a standard pair in a color you love and tack on some of these crafty details. You can dream up your own add-ons, like studs or fuzzy pompoms, or even paint your shoes with glitter for some serious twinkle toes.

ballerina girl
Sew on satin ribbons—or just fake it by
looping and tying them around your ankle.

stylish stencil
Get creative with acrylic paint and stencils.
Or make stencils from your own sketches.

earring bedazzled
Clip on the ritz by fastening oversize
vintage clip-on earrings to your shoes.

flats

These basic shoes gained a following when Audrey Hepburn
slipped into them in *Funny Face*, sporting them with capris and
oversize sunglasses. Famous for their comfort factor, flats are also
smart enough for the office and sassy enough for the dance floor.

globe-trotter logic I travel a ton—from Los Angeles to Cape Town to Vancouver. The best way to get to know a city is to walk the entire length of it, and you can't do that so well if you're wearing crazy heels. That's why I love comfy, brightly colored sneakers—I own over fifty pairs!

in a painterly way

I'm very interested in art—I love the German expressionist group Der Blaue Reiter (The Blue Rider). It was started by Kandinsky, and its members were into color's connection to the spirit—especially blue, as you can see in Franz Marc's painting here. That's possibly why my outfit reminds me of them; when I get dressed I often think about color like a painter might. I'm in art school myself, and do a bunch of multimedia paintings . . . some of which could get me into trouble! One of my favorite movies is *Beautiful Losers*, which is all about street art.

discotheque ready
Sneakers are best if you're going out to dance. I always wear them to hip-hop clubs or indie rock concerts.

KIND OF BLUE

Anna Bu | Bu the Right Thing | Hanover, Germany

I wasn't feeling like a big night out, but my friends really wanted me to meet them at a club, so I threw on an almost-all-blue outfit to indulge my mood: a baby blue t-shirt, teal leggings, and a vintage sequined jacket, plus my felted beige-and-green sneakers! Their funky but neutral color gave this look a bit of contrast.

take flight
FUN SHOES

Some shoes make you feel so great, you've just got to kick up your heels in them. From chunky work boots to major gladiator sandals, from sporty heeled sneakers to whimsical Hermes-winged wedges, your favorite footwear can be a bit impractical, as long as it allows you to be active and playful—and jump-for-joy happy.

Margerat Zhang | Shine by Three
Sydney, Australia

Zanita Whittington
Sydney, Australia

Rhiannon Leifheit | Liebemarlene Vintage
Atlanta, U.S.A.

Angela Chen | Pandaphilia
San Diego, U.S.A.

Shini Park | Park & Cube
London, U.K.

Merily Leis | Sequin Magazine
Saku, Estonia

Chantal Van Der Meijden | Cocorosa
New York City, U.S.A.

Jing Qi | Jingjing
Hanover, Germany

HEELS
take your pick

pump
An almond-shaped toe and a medium heel are always chic and flattering.

cone
Heel starts wide, then tapers down. Pant hems should almost hit the floor.

kitten heel
Playful and easy to walk in. The thin heel is less than 2 inches (5 cm) tall.

Louis
A fluted heel. Louis XIV popularized this shoe—he thought it flattered his legs.

stacked
Can be as tall as a stiletto with a heel made of leather or wood layers.

platform
An extrathick sole sneakily adds height—and acts as a shock absorber!

D'Orsay
A supersexy pump that puts the foot's arch and instep on display.

peep toe
Gives a slight flash of toe cleavage. Perfect for showing off a pedicure.

slingback
This flirty classic exposes the heel and slims the ankles and calves.

espadrille
A summer classic that's usually a mix of canvas and straw. Ties at the ankle.

cork wedge
The springy, light-colored sole matches the breezy feel of a sandal.

tie cuff
A wide ankle strap ties on. Not quite pump, and not quite bootie.

gladiator
Straps galore. Inspired by ancient warriors; some buckle at the knee.

jeweled
Complement evening wear—or make a simpler ensemble dramatic.

slide
A shoe with an open toe and back. Easy to kick off and slide back into.

geta
Japanese-style platform thongs. Most often made from wood.

cork platform
Update this flower-child staple from the 60s with an ultramodern outfit.

spectator
Two-toned, often in black and white. Started as a cricket shoe in the 1800s.

cage
Fine art for your feet, crafted from wire-like strips. Delicate yet edgy.

buckle wedge
A sandal with straps that cross and buckle shut for a punk-summer feel.

bootie
An ankle boot with a boost! Confident and fashion-forward with big sex appeal.

stiletto
Named after the dagger. Its thin heel is at least 3 inches (7.5 cm) tall.

wedge
A comfy stiletto alternative. Look for a slender wedge that won't add bulk.

demi wedge
Features a gentle sliver of a wedge. Gives just a demure bit of extra height.

ankle strap
A strap style that circles and fastens sexily around the ankle.

Mary Jane
A heel takes this schoolgirl classic into sleeker, more grown-up territory.

T-strap
A take on the Mary Jane. Choose thin straps or flesh tones to keep a long line.

cutout heel
An architectural opening detail in the heel lightens and modernizes.

clog
Traditionally designed with a clunky wooden sole and a roomy fit.

mule
A backless shoe that's an updated, more streamlined take on the clog.

lace-up boot
Don't give up your lace-up boots for summer—just get an open-toed pair!

platform wedge
A stompy choice for the modern girl on the go—stylish but tough.

sneaker
Your school-age kicks head uptown with a heel and some funky attitude.

weird and wonderful
Who said form should follow function? Expressing yourself is often more fun than pragmatism, so step up to one of these more daring ideas!

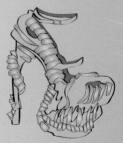

build your look

Pump Up the Tweed

Michelle Koesnadi | Glisters & Blisters
Jakarta, Indonesia

For this look, everything started with these tweed slingback pumps! I've always thought of tweed as a fabric that easily jazzes up the simplest look. A lot of times it's mistaken as formal or fussy, but it's easy to make the vibe low-key. I made these ladylike shoes more casual with a biker jacket (in more tweed!), then I added rings and a pair of sunnies, which for me is the easiest way to "upgrade" an outfit.

channeling Chanel

When I see tweed, I always think of Chanel. I know it's kind of cliché, but Chanel really is the brand I've adored ever since my mom introduced the fashion house to me when I was a child. I'm in fashion school, but I also like to unleash my creative side through drawing—it keeps me focused and relaxed during stressful days, though sometimes my artwork is fashion related. Like this watercolor I made of my favorite style icon—Coco Chanel, of course!

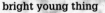

bright young thing

For this look, I wanted to prove that tweed is suitable for all occasions. I incorporated the flower-print sunnies and plastic bangles and rings to make the outfit more fun and not so formal. I stole the polka-dot headband from my mom a few years back, and I always put it on whenever I think my outfit looks stiff—it's amazing how one piece can totally change the mood of a look! Wearing white with hints of red and blue makes me feel brighter and younger, too.

revamped basics

Even though I love statement pieces, I also love working with staples—like these white jeans and navy tee. Basics allow me to get creative—I can experiment with layering, rolling, tying, safety-pinning, anything really! These white jeans were originally boot-cut, but I "skinnied" them for an updated silhouette. I tend to wear a piece for years, then when I get bored with it, I like to play around by doing some DIY work—even if it's just changing buttons.

"I love **floral** stuff, and I love wearing **colorful** items when I feel **happy** and **bright**. So I don't wear these shoes for any one special occasion, but I wear them to match and **play up my mood.**"

Yuki Lo | Oriental Sunday | Hong Kong, China

HEEL
REMIX

A pair of go-to heels doesn't have to be basic at all—you can go all-out avant garde with uncommon mesh and a chunky Lucite heel. Blend them in with diaphanous nudes as a backdrop for major jewelry, or use them as a subdued anchor for a brightly colored look. Or play off their transparency with semisheer pieces layered into a futuristic creation—plus some sparkle and knit thrown in for good measure.

Susie Lau | Style Bubble
London, U.K.

agape at agate
"This look is about drawing attention to my Brook & Lyn agate necklace, which is quite cool and can save a lazy crap outfit. This short ASOS Black skirt echoes the stones' shapes nicely."

think pink

"This sweater was a big pink Prada hug that kept me smiling through the winter. With a fluffy skirt, bright shades, blue thigh-highs, and pale heels, the powder-puff onslaught was complete."

dusky layers

"This look is an homage to some opaque draping I spied in a shop window. My take includes a sheer tee, pale green shift, metallic dress, and filmy pants, all held in place with a lace belt."

BOOTS
take your pick

classic knee-high
When wearing with a skirt or dress, let a strip of leg or stocking peek out.

slouchy
An unstructured shaft that falls into folds is disheveled-chic and bohemian.

cuff
The foldover upper is a sophisticated play on pirate-like swashbuckler style.

sneaker
An ultracasual style that laces up to the knee for a funky and unexpected vibe.

riding
A refined shape with a slim shaft that's flattering for any body type.

laced riding
Ankle-cinching laces make the definitive riding boot more informal.

harness
A mix between cowboy and biker styles, with straps and a metal ring.

biker
Take a ride on the wild side with chunky, buckled-up black leather boots.

cowboy
Don these to kick up dust or embrace your inner free-spirited cowgirl.

combat
Adapted from military gear, with serious traction for a tough impression.

hiking
Often leather and ripstop canvas. Outdoorsy for adventurous girls.

work
No-nonsense boots often with a steel toe that protects in risky situations.

kiltie
A fringed detail dangles from under the laces onto the toe box.

Victorian
Time-travel to a ladylike era with a curved heel and covered buttons.

gaiter
A dapper-looking separate piece buckles around the shaft of the boot.

moon
Insulated and water-resistant for winter wanders and snow-angel making.

clog
The Danish classic is a little edgier in boot form. A bit bulky for petite legs.

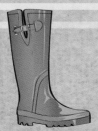

rubber
Adds a countryside vibe to muddy summers and slushy winters alike.

demi wedge
Lifts you just above the slush or rain, while staying totally comfortable.

hidden wedge
Maintains a fuss-free sensibility while secretly adding height.

wedge
A modern style that's as sassy as a stiletto but much more practical.

foldover
Excess leather encircles the boot, folded over for a layered look.

over the knee
Draws eyes to the thighs. Pair with tall socks and short, flirty skirts.

convertible
Like buying multiple pairs of boots at once! Zip off pieces to transform.

laced back
A slightly medieval imagining of a classic flat boot. Tuck jeans inside.

cutout
A pattern of cutouts gives peeks of skin—or perhaps colorful tights.

huarache
Interwoven strips of leather create a breathable and textural pattern.

low
A quintessential boot, but shorter so it doesn't disrupt trousers' silhouette.

Chelsea
Elastic gores create a clean fit under pants. The Beatles made them iconic.

shoe
A modernized cowboy boot that's cut off at the ankle. Menswear-inspired.

open flat
A simple, flat boot with an open toe is playful and funky for warmer months.

desert
A flat, ankle-high, lace-up boot, often in suede. Borrowed from the boys.

field
A classic lace-up ankle boot that's basic while adding a slight edge.

knit
Cozy, sweatery boots with a sturdy sole that lets them go outside.

sock cuff
A stretchy, knit band attached inside is a snuggly, protective layer.

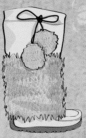

moccasin
All the Indian-princess charm of a flat moccasin, but warm for winter.

mukluk
An old-school Inuit style that's been adopted by ski bunnies worldwide.

shearling
Nothing insulates as well as natural wool lining. A soft, chunky shape.

platform
A disco-age icon. Look for streamlined modern styles, or go chunky and retro.

go-go
Let the vinyl gleam as you shimmy to Motown hits. Pair with a minidress.

heeled
A leg-lengthening alternative to a flat boot for petites who want a bit of lift.

stiletto
A spikelike heel elevates and dresses up the traditional boot.

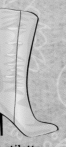

strappy
A funky cousin to a strappy sandal. Gives a gladiator-style edge.

thigh-high
A fitted, superhigh style that infuses any look with bad-girl sex appeal.

take me to Tokyo

I first discovered the Miu Miu shoes that I'm wearing in this look when I was visiting Tokyo—easily my favorite city, and my favorite place to shop. Japanese designers have really informed my aesthetic; the clothes are so avant-garde and deconstructed. Plus, Tokyo is a great place to scout for additions to another ever-growing collection of mine—Japanese toys!

big-time shoe fetish

I believe shoes should be like miniature sculptures, and I'm lucky to have a collection of pairs that I consider to be art. When I made sketches for my shoe line (pictured hanging in the trees here!), I drew upon my closet for inspiration—like these bowtie Chanel booties, hot-pink lace-up Pradas, and brown spectator Marni platforms. For me, designing starts with being a fan.

style reruns

When I was brainstorming for my shoe line, I watched tons of *Dynasty* clips. I love the fussy, gaudy details—the sequins and bows, the wide shoulders and drapery. I'm also a big *Twin Peaks* fan, which I think you can see in this look. The oversize cardigan and the dress's super-saturated colors evoke the cozy-eerie look of early '90s David Lynch.

build your look
Badass Booties

Jane Aldridge | Sea of Shoes | Dallas, U.S.A.

I put this look together to announce a line of shoes I created for Urban Outfitters. I was excited to share my designs, so I wore some of my favorite shoes—these awesome Miu Miu ankle booties! They're supersoft suede and covered with studs in a swirly motif. I paired them with a painterly Dries Van Noten dress, a long cardi, and a ram's head–bedecked belt.

ACCESSORIES

HANDBAGS
take your pick

foldover clutch
A small, bendable bag with a cutout shape. Unfold to carry by the handle.

frame clutch
This structured clutch is often secured with a kiss-lock clasp.

pouch
Often made of silk or satin. Big enough for an evening out's must-have items.

muff
Hands stay cozy while stuff stays hidden in pouches in the fur lining.

carpet
A 1900s need for cheap luggage led to bags made from old carpet bits.

doctor's
This bag lends a professional but vintage vibe to an ensemble.

attaché
Your workbag can make a statement. Look for special fabrics or details.

bowling
A versatile, sporty bag constructed of sturdy materials like leather or canvas.

structured
This satchel puts a professional click in your walk. Modern and put-together.

slouchy satchel
A functional but relaxed, slightly saucy take on a structured satchel.

chain strap
The delicate metal strap can often be found on a dainty quilted purse.

baguette
With a body wider than it is tall, this bag rests just under the upper arm.

crescent
This bag's curved, graceful form evokes the shape of a half-moon.

hobo
This short-strapped and slouchy shoulder bag is a boho standard.

drawstring
Backpack-style straps and a top closure that cinches for security.

saddle
These bags inspired by cowboy culture hit the streets in the 1970s.

tooled
A method of leather carving creates a special, organic-looking pattern.

medicine
This tiny sack is just the right size for healing herbs—or a cell phone.

basket
A design inspired by artisanal crafts with woven, leather, and wood materials.

straw
Natural fibers, an open weave, and a roomy interior make for a summer go-to.

wristlet
A short strap allows
this clutch-style bag
to dangle daintily
from the wrist.

envelope
Constructed like a
paper envelope with
a flap and a sleek,
slim shape.

minaudière
An evening clutch
with a hard shell
that's usually
sparkle studded.

box
First crafted of clear
Lucite in the 1950s.
At once modern
and ladylike.

train case
This sturdy, retro
case allows makeup
or delicate items
to travel safely.

camera
You take your
camera everywhere;
why not carry its
case as a fun bag?

dome
A rectangular shape
with a flat bottom,
round top, and two
short handles.

hat box
This shape can
make your look retro
and refined, even if
it doesn't hold hats.

takeout
A small, whimsical
riff on a takeout
carton. Often made
of bright satin.

circle
Cleverly conceived
for a mod, cultivated
look. Pair with a
simple silhouette.

tote
A classic carryall
that can go from the
gym to the farmer's
market to the mall.

shopper
A shoulder strap
leaves hands free
to explore hangers
and shelves.

backpack
Sturdy with double
shoulder straps. A
classic, whether old-
school or high-style.

sling
Fits the body like
a backpack, but
with just a single
wide strap.

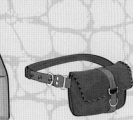

fanny pack
Stash essentials in
this fun bag that
sits on the hips, and
go hands-free.

bucket
A roomy bag based
on the most basic
container shape can
hold all you need.

flat
A slender bag that
fits across the body
is just right when
you're on the move.

hipster
Often tasseled and
made of knit wool
or a patchwork of
colorful fabrics.

fishing creel
A straw bag with
leather details and
a foldover top that
buckles shut.

surplus
Military gear bags
are made to stand
up to wear and tear.
Try adding patches.

messenger
A rectangular shape
rests on the back,
secured by a wide,
padded strap.

weekend
Large enough for a
weekend's worth of
essentials—without
a bulky shape.

duffle
The cylindrical, soft
shape comes in
travel-size and
mini versions.

trimmed in roses
Buy, craft, or salvage silk flowers, then glue
or sew them along the clutch's edge.

pearl-strand strap
String a pearl chain or necklace under the
clutch's flap, and carry it as a crossbody.

studly style
Lend a little edge to this ladylike staple
by poking earring studs through the flap.

CLUTCH REMIX

Every girl needs a basic clutch—whether coyly tucked against the body or carried right
front and center, it adds a little arm candy and sweetens up any outfit. Not to mention, it's
the best way to carry minimal stuff with maximum style. Of course, you will have to pack
more wisely—and, most importantly, remember not to leave it in the cab.

tied with a bow
Sew or glue a wide satin ribbon inside your clutch to transform it into a wristlet.

zipped up
Line structural details with zippers (the glue gun is your friend) for a more raw look.

get a grip
Sick of clutching that clutch? Close the flap over a chain loop to make a simple handle.

clutch
These cute little carriers are on the market in just about any style, shape, or color. Go the unexpected route with a unique fabric like brocade, or an unusual shape like a triangle. Just make sure it fits your phone, wallet, and keys.

build your look

CUBE BAG

Clara Campelo | Zebratrash | Rio Branco, Brazil

This box-shaped bag was a surprise gift from my godmother. It has a chain that can be worn as a bracelet, and it's made of checkered leather. There are so many different colors—I can carry it with anything, and it's still the biggest attraction in any outfit. I love its unconventional design—it's such an artistic creation!

heat-wave minimalism
Nature often limits or expands my creativity, because where I live it's very hot. The heat makes me a minimalist—little touches like the bag, purple sunglasses, striped hat, and brightly colored nail polish really complete an outfit when you can't wear a lot. The earring is just a pendant that I put on a hook and wear all on its own. Who needs two?

laundry day
These silk pants aren't usually wrinkled, but in this look I've just dug them out of my clothes hamper. I love how being all wadded up gives them a "trashed" air. Also, these pants were my sister's, and she lives in Spain now, so they are a souvenir from happy times. I sewed them to fit me but left a bump on the back to make a different silhouette.

fashion as architecture

This outfit's textures and colors remind me of buildings that glitter or create illusions with external lighting, like the colors in Frank Gehry's Hotel Marqués de Riscal in Elciego, Spain, or the shimmering metal "scales" on his Guggenheim Museum in Bilbao, Spain. The bag and pants reflect little bursts of light, and the top has a speckled pattern, too. I think these fabrics and shapes are very '80s, and I love the '80s.

NECKLACES & BRACELETS
take your pick

pearls
Gives the feel of an elegant heirloom (even if it's not!) to add a dose of class.

collar
A solid, inflexible ring that sits atop the collarbone and has an open back.

choker
Closely encircles the neck for a sexy look. Often made of bejeweled ribbon.

chain
Chunky links form a necklace that is modern, tough, and makes a statement.

rope
A superlong strand of any material can be doubled or tripled to shorten.

layered
The look of multiple necklaces, but all in one and joined by a single clasp.

fringe
Delicate, drapey fringe creates a slightly edgy and artful appeal.

woven
Braided or twisted strands of metal and fabric are at once folksy and fine.

lariat
A single strand that secures by forming a loop, rather than clasping shut.

beaded
Usually a vintage, kitschy costume piece made of chunky baubles.

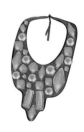

bib
A decorated fabric piece covers most of the chest. Inspired by tribal jewelry.

pendant
A stone, gem, or charm hangs from a chain or cord as the necklace's focus.

drop
An extension forms a Y shape and dangles coyly along the collarbone.

cameo
Portraits carved on shell, gem, or stone create dreamy, figurative motifs.

logo
A pendant that spells out a name, title, or statement. Bring on the bling.

pocket watch
This tiny clock dangles from a long chain. A distinctive, refined keepsake.

cluster
Try collecting a few pendants you love to create a special custom cluster.

spaced bead
Beads are placed and knotted so they can't move for a lasting composition.

locket
A sentimental symbol. Opens to reveal a photo of your choice.

tennis
This iconic, luxe piece features an endless row of tiny, sparkling diamonds.

hinged bangle
A bangle with a hinge can fit slightly tighter than one that slides on.

ID
An engraved plate features a name or a message for a personalized touch.

link
Interconnecting loops of any shape move slinkily about on the wrist.

stacked bangles
Make some noise by piling a jangly stack of narrow bangles onto any look.

filigree
A graceful piece with a delicate, vine-like pattern. Usually silver.

charm
A linked chain has plenty of places to attach trinkets from your travels.

multistrand
Several strands of varied or the same material clasp together as one.

wraparound
Circles the wrist several times before snapping or clasping shut.

wide cuff
An extranoticeable, armor-inspired piece with an Egyptian edge.

Jane Aldridge | Sea of Shoes
Dallas, U.S.A.

cuff
A stiff piece curves around the wrist. Look for unexpected materials like vinyl.

hammered
A metalworking technique creates a glimmery, dimpled appearance.

arm band
A coil or cuff that fits around the upper arm rather than the wrist.

laced
Usually made of sturdy leather. A bit ancient Roman, a bit rock 'n' roll.

geometric
A bracelet with hard angles can give a sharp-edged finish to an outfit.

Celtic
A traditional weaving-knot pattern symbolizes timelessness.

safety pin
Utilitarian pins become fun and whimsical with beads and elastic.

woven
Try natural fibers with neutral colors, like hemp. Earthy and easygoing.

The Squid Was Telling Me Dirty Jokes

Jane Aldridge | Sea of Shoes | Dallas, U.S.A.

My mom and I have a large collection of animal-themed jewelry, and we love adding to our menagerie. So when we saw this squid necklace—made by Paris-based designer Hanna Bernhard—it was obsession at first sight. It's a work of art in its own right—I love its frenzied, detailed beadwork and playful tentacles.

underwater dreaming

I love underwater life; that's why my blog is called Sea of Shoes. I'm especially obsessed with the arapaiama. It's one of the largest freshwater fish in the world, and it's covered with large red scales. They seem so powerful and mysterious. And so prehistoric. They appear in my dreams a lot. Wouldn't it be cool to have a crazy piece of jewelry featuring the arapaima?

West African inspiration

To me this necklace echoes the symbolic use of animals in so much African art—where creatures are more like characters in a story. The necklace is so large that it resembles a dance plate in a ceremonial costume, and the intricacy of its beading reminds me of Yoruba pieces, like this crown and cushion.

fish on display

The scale and impact of this statement necklace really makes it stand on its own, so I wanted to keep the rest of the outfit fairly simple. The plain shape and fabric of this red-and-orange Jelly Garcia dress ended up being a perfect backdrop. I'm also wearing a gold sequin bandeau, which seems to pick up the jewelry's beaded texture, and a pair of Gucci heels—I love the shape of this shoe.

Tuuli Jurgenson | Fallie's Scrapbook
Tartu, Estonia

Chantal Van Der Meijden | Cocorosa
New York City, U.S.A.

Sigurbjorg Stefansdottir | Sibba Stef
Kopavogur, Iceland

Ilanka Verhoeven | Fashionnerdic
Rotterdam, Netherlands

Jane Aldridge | Sea of Shoes
Dallas, U.S.A.

Sandra Hagelstam | 5 Inch And Up
London, U.K.

Aurélia Scheyé | Fashion Is a Playground
Paris, France

Andrea Bomo | Paris Most Wanted
Paris, France

wearable art
JEWELRY

Transform an average outfit into a chic ensemble with the right jewelry. From thread-thin cascading chains to chunky plastic-goes-tribal necklaces, from '70s-esque feathers to outrageous cocktail rings, you can combine eye-catching materials for intriguing juxtaposition—or sport solo pieces for minimalist sparkle.

RINGS & EARRINGS
take your pick

band
Simple, effortless.
Can be engraved
with decorative trim
or a message.

box
A rectangular gem
in a bezel setting
(a raised frame that
encases the stone).

mosaic
Shards of glass or
stone like turquoise
are pieced into a
geometric design.

blossom
Frilly and sweet.
A tiny, twinkling
stone is often inlaid
among the petals.

solitaire
Timeless. Try in
surprising stones to
keep engagement
rumors at bay.

channel
Gemstones sparkle
from a groove in the
band for under-
stated elegance.

stack
Thin or chunky,
bling encrusted or
bare. Buy a set
or mix your own.

scatter
A wide and
dramatic band with
irregularly placed
gemstones.

dome
The band arches
into a bubble shape.
In metal, wood, or
playful plastic.

cluster
Jewels or beads are
gathered in a loose
configuration. Some
even dangle!

oval
An oblong stone in
a prong or bezel
setting. Slightly
antique looking.

knuckle
Arty and a little
intimidating, this
metal ring is cast to
fit over the knuckle.

double knuckle
A thin metal bar
bridges two bands
for a tough yet
delicate look.

coil
Often in snake,
rope, or braid
motifs. Creates a
multiband effect.

cocktail
If it's whimsical,
wildly oversize, and
completes your look,
it's a cocktail ring.

scarab
A symbol of
protection and luck
that was adopted
from ancient Egypt.

signet
An engraved ring
showcasing crests,
initials, or other
personal insignia.

cartouche
Carved with
Egyptian symbols
and glyphs. Like an
ancient ID bracelet.

armor
A simple band
connected to
delicate chains.
Slightly medieval.

button
A round shape larger than a stud, often in enamel or precious metals.

pavé
Tiny, allover stones make a surface appear "paved" with sparkle.

stud
These prong-backed cut jewels put a subtle, tasteful glint in your earlobes.

chandelier
Beads or gems dangle in tiers or layers for movement and shimmer.

drop
A prominent charm or gem hangs from a chain or vertical arrangement.

girandole
A French design featuring three extensions from a main gem or stud.

costume
Styles that clip onto the earlobe let you experiment without the commitment.

disc
A flat, round piece dangles from a wire. Often constructed of wood and metal.

hoop
The circular shape fits through the ear. Size determines if it's preppy or blingy.

gypsy hoop
A hoop shape is mounted to a stud so that the open circle faces forward.

captive bead
A small hoop is secured with a tiny bead. Not just for your ears!

cuff
Fits over the ear's cartilage like a bracelet instead of piercing through.

dangly
Whether dressy or wacky, they'll grab attention. Can be up to shoulder-length.

stacked
Layered beads can have a bohemian or arts-and-crafts feel. Design your own!

spike
A choice that's sure to make any look tougher, edgier, and more modern.

pull through
A delicate wire is angled to stay in place without an earring back.

plug
A cylindrical shape that causes the wearer's pierced opening to widen.

whimsical
Tiny studs let you add a dose of silliness without going over the top.

EARRINGS
REMIX

Everybody needs at least one risky, in-your-face piece of jewelry that makes any outfit plain unstoppable. These ultralong feathered red earrings do just that—whether worn as a pair with an equally textured fur vest and utility fanny pack, in the singular to balance out a megahigh side ponytail, or as the wild-card accessory that keeps a girlish look from getting too sugary sweet.

Michelle Haswell | Kingdom of Style
London, U.K.

Mad Max style
"This is really an everday look for me. I'd wear it to run errands, but with a few pieces to make the jeans more interesting—like my bag, which attaches to the leg, and the feather earrings."

channeling 1989
"I wore this for my birthday night. I'd turned thirty-seven and we went to an old-school rock club—hence the PVC, army-style boots, leather, feathers, and asymmetrical details."

cute, not cutesy
"I'm definitely exploring my feminine side with this look. Pretty bows and pink aren't my style, but it's good to move outside your comfort zone. The earrings help give it a rougher texture."

EYEWEAR
take your pick

small round
A bookish but hip style worn by John Lennon. Best on heart-shaped faces.

half-rim
Without a bottom rim, these frames won't overpower delicate features.

clip on
Keep out rays and go for funky '80s style by clipping shades onto glasses.

aviator
Whether wire or plastic, they're a summer staple. Best on square faces.

Wayfarer style
Understated and effortlessly cool. Great on oval and heart-shaped faces.

shield
Just one large front lens can take a basic outfit into an avant-garde future.

wraparound
Whether chic or sporty, the shaded lens extends to protect at sides.

oval
With movie-star appeal, but not so big that small faces can't wear them.

oversize round
Ultraglamorous, this style's curves will balance a square face's angles.

butterfly
Widens from the nosepiece outward. Flatters oval and heart shapes.

curved cat's eye
Upward-tilting, curved frames will flatter angular or narrow faces.

heart
A fanciful style that can keep your look from taking itself too seriously.

angled cat's eye
A cat's-eye style that's sharp enough to work for oval or round faces.

geometric
Crazy, attention-grabbing shades reference B-boy style at its best.

trapezoid
An angled shape that narrows toward the bottom. Great for round faces.

flat top
A straight-across top ridge infuses just a touch of hip-hop appeal.

rectangle
An eternally nerdy-chic style, especially in black plastic frames.

oversize square
Round faces can get away with an oversize style if it's a bit angular.

sleek geek

Here I'm combining polished, glossy items with androgynous separates to make the nerdy outfit more sexy and put together. These rectangular black frames and the white button-down shirt are made glamorous by a black satin bubble skirt (one of my favorites), black tights, and secondhand wingtip heels—I exploded with delight when I found them!

tribute to the man

I have a friend who jokingly calls me Madame Lagerfeld because of my l'amour for structured black and white, so I decided to pay proper homage to Karl Lagerfeld himself with this look.

heirloom touches

I remember my mother wearing this cardigan when I was a child, and I found the beading on it absolutely fascinating. My grandmother gave me the cameo pendant, and I made it into an earring, which I usually prefer to pin onto my clothes instead of my ear. The tie is actually a satin sash that used to be on an old blouse of mine. I felt the sash and the pendant worked well together—they're both not quite what you think they are, so they can sneak about together in their fakery!

LIBRARIAN CHIC

Tahti Syrjala | Cork, Ireland

I like to sport interesting glasses, because I figure if I have to wear them I might as well try and make a statement! I wear these angular, black-frame Tommy Hilfiger glasses on an every-other-day basis. Whenever I don somber, serious outfits like this I feel like I should be somewhat dignified and aloof (maybe shushing someone!), but it doesn't last very long—I like laughing too much to care about looking haute constantly.

gotta have 'em
SUNNIES

From mirrored aviators to candy-colored plastic frames, from dramatic flip-tops to mottled tortoiseshell, the world really is your oyster when it comes to sunglass style. When investing in a pair, be sure that they flatter your face shape, work well with just about any outfit, and make you feel like a movie star every time you put them on. (Now, whether you're starring in a nonstop-action thriller, an indie sleeper, or a classic film-noir flick . . . that's up to you.)

Raez Argulla | Cheap Thrills
Winnipeg, Canada

Cindy Ko | Cindiddy
Hong Kong, China

Maria Confer | Lulu Letty
Court Brighton, U.S.A.

Alexandra Pereira Romero | Lovely Pepa
Vigo, Spain

Laura Allard-Fleischl | Luna Supernova
Auckland, New Zealand

Marianne Theodorsen | Styledevil
Oslo, Norway

Jessica Virgin | Vintage Virgin
Montrose, U.S.A.

Iris Gravemaker | Fashion Zen
Hilversum, Netherlands

HATS
take your pick

cadet
Military inspired and practical with a flat crown and a short, stiff brim.

baseball
An adjustable, sporty staple adopted from American baseball.

newsboy
A full, paneled cap with a button on top. Go for a tweed version in winter.

bucket
This hat's soft, foldable shape and shading brim make it perfect for travel.

floppy
Use it to top off a floral dress and tall boots for an earthy, '70s-inspired look.

cowboy
Originated in the American West, with a wide brim for the sunny plains.

fedora
With a creased crown and a short brim. First worn by ladies, not gents!

porkpie
A short, flat crown and narrow brim. Brings a jovial, playful element.

visor
A wraparound band with a full brim protects your eyes from the sun.

bowler
Immortalized by Charlie Chaplin, it was introduced in the 1850s.

top
A dandy one-time staple that's now hard to rock. Be brave and creative.

pillbox
A smart, flat-crowned hat that gained high-fashion status in the 1960s.

beanie
Usually knit, this hat is flexible and closely fitted to keep in warmth.

boule
A mix between a cloche and a beanie. Fitted and usually made of molded felt.

turban
Sometimes wrapped and tied, sometimes crafted on a base for on-and-off ease.

trapper
Fur-lined flannel or leather protects ears whether on a sled or in a plane.

chullo
A Peruvian and Bolivian take on a winter hat in cozy, patterned wool.

snood
A fabric or crocheted pouch can protect a glamorous 'do.

fascinator
Deliciously frivolous. Sits jauntily atop the crown. Use pins!

sculptural
Nothing can elevate or top off an ensemble like fine art for your head!

veiled
The fishnet veil is gothy or glamorous, depending on how you style it.

trucker
With a breathable mesh back and a slightly raised front crown.

ivy cap
A nearly flat cap with a fabric-covered brim. Lends a tomboy feel.

bibi
A shallow hat, often with embellishment, sits flashily just a touch off center.

beret
Soft but voluminous, the beret is at once whimsical and seriously French.

cloche
A flapper favorite with a fitted bell shape. Usually made of felt.

Funeka Ngwevela | The Quirky Stylista
Johannesburg, South Africa

sun
To block the rays and stay cool, a hat woven of straw is just the thing.

boater
A summer hat with flat crown and brim that's often trimmed with ribbon.

coon
Whether fake or real, it adds a little countryside flair to a basic outfit.

ushanka
Made of fur, with flaps that fold up or down to withstand a Russian winter.

platter
The dramatic, superwide brim lends a luxe and regal air.

FEDORA REMIX

Beat the heat and look chic with a borrowed-from-the-news-beat fedora. This classic topper can jazz up any outfit and occasion—wear it for a hot summer date with the dude and the dog, for making a cameo at a hip gallery event, or even just for a lazy Sunday brunch out in the sun.

Aimee Song | Song of Style
San Francisco, U.S.A.

day at the dog park
"This outfit was for a family date with my boyfriend and our adorable 'son' Charcoal. The fedora was the finishing piece with the blousy top, flirty skirt, and chunky heels."

hitting the scene
"I wanted to look presentable but not overdone for an art gallery event. So I complemented the fringed cardigan with the fedora and a black top and vintage leather shorts underneath."

Sunday brunch
"To offset the monochrome of the black asymmetrical jumpsuit and black wedges, I added my fedora and topped it off with a sparkly headband above the brim."

build your look
THE GIRL IN THE GOLDEN BERET

Xiaoxi (Nancy) Zhang | Sea of Fertility | Berlin, Germany

This handmade hat was a sweet gift from my friend Shan Shan. It was the first autumn I spent in Berlin. Outside it was amazingly beautiful, and the hat's shape and colors reminded me of fall. So I gathered garments in all the warm colors of the hat and then used a few cool ones to make a look with an autumn feeling. Then I added these clown shoes—they make the whole outfit more fantastic.

daily portraits

I'm an illustrator, and every day I draw an outfit. Often I draw my own look, usually inspired by a movie, painting, poem, or novel. (My blog is actually named after Yukio Mishima's *Sea of Fertility* tetralogy; its mix of modern and traditional Japanese themes has really informed my personal aesthetic.) I've drawn so many of these outfits now—they're little self-portraits for me to look back on, and to see how my fashion and illustration style has changed.

Francophile cinephile

This hat is shaped like a beret, and as cliché as it is, one of the reasons I like it so much is that it reminds me of French New Wave films. I love Godard's *Une femme est une femme* and *Vivre sa vie*—I am inspired by the playful, simple colors and chic shapes that Danish actress Anna Karina wears in these films.

stripes meet dots

Decorative painting inspired this outfit—especially that of Austrian artist Gustav Klimt, who uses organic shapes and patterns on an irregular grid, all in warm, decadent colors. The graphic stripes in this skirt and vest and the dots in the hat and shirt all combine to look like a Klimt painting. I am also inspired by Japanese installation artist Yayoi Kusama, who covers the world in bright polka dots—her yellow, spotted pumpkins look like my hat!

BELTS & HAIR THINGS

take your pick

skinny
Use it to add a zing of unexpected color, or break up a solid dress or long shirt.

ring
A versatile style that closes over dresses or skirts with a metal ring.

sash
Often fabric or suede. One end pulls through an open buckle.

camp
Made of canvas with a metal clasp. Utilitarian with a bit of Boy Scout casual.

post
Pegs fit through the belt's holes to hold it in place without a belt buckle.

wraparound
Get a slouchy, layered look with a belt that winds around the waist.

double buckle
Sits at the natural waist, giving the effect of a modern-day corset.

waist cinch
Made of wide elastic, it's perfect for nipping in a dress or tunic top.

angled
A 1980s style that gives a nod to superheros. Makes a V shape in front.

obi
A wide stretch of fabric wraps and knots at front kimono-style.

beaded
A belt with a handcrafted feel adds an artisanal quality to your look.

double ring
Weave an end through one ring, then the other for total adjustability.

woven
Braided strips of leather or cloth macrame add textural interest.

grommet
Decorative whipstitching tones down military-inspired grommets.

studded
Metal studs or spikes give any outfit a tough, punky counterpoint.

pouch
Look for modern, sassy incarnations of the old-school fanny pack.

Western
Leather buckles with an engraved metal plate add cowboy swagger.

disc
Leather discs, often with hammered metal detailing, sit low on the hips.

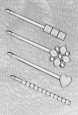

bobby pin
Can be plain to blend in with hair or embellished to add sparkle.

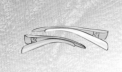

alligator clip
Often made of silver metal. Curved to rest against the shape of the head.

barrette
A decorative band conceals the metal clasp. Look for special materials.

stick barrette
A sticklike piece threads through a molded curve. Great for ponytails.

hair fork
This two-pronged stick holds a bun or a French twist right in place.

comb
Secures front pieces off the face while offering delicate Victorian allure.

clip
These don't hold much hair, but they superbly anchor flyaways and frizz.

elastic band
Basics get an upgrade with baubles and other pretty additions.

scrunchie
A fabric covering on an elastic band protects hair in classic 1990s style.

claw
A hinged style with talon-like teeth can be found in large or small versions.

hair sticks
Insert two sticks at different angles, and they'll hold surprisingly well.

bow
A little-girl bow barrette can add whimsy to a more grown-up look.

feathered
A dreamy accent that's a blend of '40s-chic and nature lover.

headband
A horseshoe shape that sits across the head and rests behind the ears.

head wrap
Try tying a scarf or piece of fabric around your head as a headband.

hippie
Circles the forehead in flower-child style. Look for braided leather or suede.

circlet
Infuse your look with fairy-princess intrigue. Rests around the crown.

headdress
Draping, ornate chain- or beadwork is fanciful and a little dark.

sweatband
A stretchy terry-cloth band that makes a look fresh and sporty.

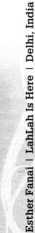

Esther Fanai | LahLah Is Here | Delhi, India

BELT
REMIX

Belts first hit the scene as the best way to keep up your britches, but these days, they're as statement-making as they are practical. Use a simple skinny one to add unexpected preppy texture to a summery dress, to give definition to a bravely patterned jumpsuit, or tether a multilayered look.

Constance Phillips | Constance-Victoria
London, U.K.

sweet child o' mine
"The belt was used here to add more detail to the empire waistline. I love the contrast of the delicate floral dress with the chunky necklaces and the leathers of the belt and bag."

a taming touch
"I wanted to use the belt to pull in the waist of this vintage jumpsuit, giving it a much more flattering silhouette. It also helps break up the loud floral print a little!"

home chic home
"I piled on layers of different fabrics to make a mix of textures. The belt is then used as a decorative item to draw the eye. I would wear this out any day or even around the house."

I AM WEARING A BOX. ON. MY. HEAD!

Tavi Gevinson | Style Rookie | Chicago, U.S.A.

I once got a fancy gift in this box—it has a perfect shape and is covered in tiny black, brown, and gold lines. Since it's just paper, I stuck a giant hairclip through it and wore it on my head. The hat itself looks like some kind of candy treat, so the rest of the outfit obviously became about licorice.

candy geometry

The hat's lines went well with the ribbon belt and striped bag, and the jewelry—all made of round beads—helped balance the sharp shapes in the stripes and dress print. Each item incorporates a different candy I was inspired by—be it by way of colors, shapes, or patterns.

feminist fashion

I'm always looking at zines and *Sassy* magazines from the '90s—*Sassy* was a cult teen monthly that had a lot of savvy, snarky advice. And I'm really into Kathleen Hanna, of feminist punk and girlpop bands Bikini Kill and Le Tigre. People may think it's weird that someone who likes fashion self-identifies as feminist, but being into style doesn't mean compromising yourself for what others think looks right. For me, it means wearing what I want. And that's a pretty feminist thing for a girl to do.

" IT SEEMS BORING TO ME TO PURSUE THE TYPICAL IDEA OF BEAUTY, BECAUSE THAT IS THE EASIEST AND THE MOST OBVIOUS WAY TO SEE THE WORLD. IT'S MORE CHALLENGING TO LOOK AT THE OTHER SIDE! " CINDY SHERMAN

Treacy treats

This headpiece was inspired by milliner Philip Treacy. His pieces are over-the-top fantastical creations . . . This swirly one looks like a meringue. And, of course, everybody knows I love anything Rei Kawakubo does for Comme Des Garçons—especially the looks for fall 2009. I like to think that my dress's pattern and the overall proportions of the outfit reference this collection.

"Hats and headpieces are a final **quirky flourish** to many of my outfits. I was drawn to the **rich tones** of the feathers in this headpiece—they remind me of **autumn leaves**."

Rebecca Stice | The Clothes Horse | Fort Monroe, U.S.A.

GLOVES & SCARVES
take your pick

mittens
Bring some cheerful, childlike nostalgia to your casual wintertime look.

knitted
A soft and stretchy ribbed cuff keeps the cold from sneaking in.

convertible
The mitten-style top keeps fingertips cozy, but folds down for dexterity.

wrist warmers
A tube covers the wrist and knuckles, but exposes the thumb and fingers.

fingerless
A tough-girl classic that sets fingers free. Look for leather or lace.

finger cuffs
Covers just the knuckles. Adds a sassy swagger, but not much warmth!

wrist
Dips low along the wrist for a peek of skin from under a coat sleeve.

laced
If it's too cold to show off a corset, try gloves that echo the sexy styling.

driving
Perforation and a center opening allow for flexibility and ventilation.

opera
Extends past the elbow for ultimate elegance. Try in velvet or satin.

half
A short glove that covers fingers and knuckles but leaves the wrist bare.

wrist cuff
Adds a festive, luxe feel whether on a bare arm or at the end of a coat sleeve.

crocheted
A pretty and refined open-knit glove that evokes ladylike picnics by the lake.

snow
Pull on thick and intensely insulated gloves before making snowballs.

ear muffs
Fluffy knitted or fur ear covers attached by a band over the head.

ski band
A stretchy, sporty option that fits low across the ears and forehead.

hood
Add a gracefully draping hood to make any outfit more elegant.

neck warmer
Fits just around the neck to keep you warm without the bulk of a scarf.

kerchief
Knot a cotton or silk scarf at your collar to add spunky, playful spark.

infiniti
A circular scarf goes on over the head for all-encompassing, cushy comfort.

pull-through
One end secures by pulling through a hole in the other to stay snug.

pom pom
Whimsical pom poms give a playful tone to a warm and functional piece.

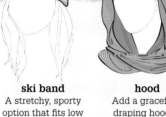

fringed
Frayed or fringed edges can be chic but easygoing, too. Try in a pattern.

boa
Style a feather or fur boa to be cheeky and risqué, ultra-classy, or both!

tippet
Circles the upper arms to cut a slight chill but still puts an outfit on display.

stole
Look lavish with glamorous, chunky fur draped around your shoulders.

wrap
Use this oversize piece in place of a light jacket, or as an extra lush scarf.

shawl
Pair a cozy shawl with a modern outfit to avoid a full-on grandma look.

fichu
A delicate capelike piece used to drape daintily over a dress or blouse.

build your look
Afternoon Tea Party

Roz Jana | Clothes, Cameras, and Coffee | West Midlands, U.K.

I inherited a beautiful big box of vintage gloves from my great-grandmother—this teal mesh pair is one of my favorites. I chose them to go with this 1950s dress as they matched the shades of the dress perfectly, then I added slouchy vintage Brettles stockings, thrifted pearls, and Topshop shoes. I'm particularly fond of tea parties with bone china and fabulous cakes, and this look definitely reflects that aesthetic!

vintage lineage

These gloves are quite nostalgic for me, as I have come to know my late relatives through the items that they left me. Be it my great-grandma's gorgeous gloves displayed in a vanity case next to my bed, or my great grand-dad's tail coat hanging outside my room, these clothes have helped me to understand my family. I am also very lucky that many family members were great hoarders—it has made for an amazing, almost sentimental vintage collection.

homage to Erdem

This 1950s dress reminds me so much of an Erdem-style pattern. He designs beautiful, slightly anachronistic prints that echo the past, but that look slightly digitized, like blurry floral prints. Being a big fan of his work, but not yet in a position to afford it, I was very happy to find a frock that slightly mimics his signature look!

fairy-tale inspiration

This look was not exactly inspired by a style icon—however, I was told that my wrinkled silk stockings emulated those of frumpy British sitcom character Nora Batty! Generally, I draw inspiration from film icons like Moira Shearer—I love the drama and saturated hues of *The Red Shoes*—and fairy tales by Hans Christian Andersen, like *The Princess and the Pea*. Sometimes I even make outfits based on children's stories. Literature is such a rich source of inspiration for me.

SCARF REMIX

News flash, darlings: A scarf isn't just for your neck! This is one swath of fabric that you can wear dozens of ways, whether as an unexpected extra or a garment in its own right. Pick one you love and reconsider its potential—would it provide enough coverage if worn as a halter, or is it tiny enough to make a dainty wrist cuff? Then start playing, stat!

elegant obi belt
Fold the scarf in half and wrap it around your waist, then twist and tuck the ends.

hippie headscarf
Give off a modern-bohemian vibe by tying it around your head and letting the ends flow.

braided and wrapped
Add extra texture to your winter wrappings by weaving multiple scarves together.

fringed scarf

A fringed wool-blend scarf is really basic, and gives you lots of options—because, really, what's more versatile than a simple fabric rectangle? Be aware that for some looks, you'll want to practice wrapping, draping, and pinning before debuting it in public.

loose but belted
To add dimension to a body-skimming look, drape the scarf over the neck and belt it.

updated sarong
Wrap the scarf around your waist, gather it artfully into pleats, and then pin in place.

toga top
Start with a tube-top shape, then draw the fabric over your shoulder and tuck in back.

"This Spanish-looking **vintage shawl**
is just grannyish enough to be cool—and
there are a **million ways** to wear it."

Sandra Hagelstam | 5 Inch and Up | London, U.K.

UNDERPINNINGS

BRA BASICS

One of the most essential components of your outfit is one people don't even see—your bra! Still, the right fit is crucial to achieving a shapely silhouette. When shopping for a bra, you'll want to know your band size (that's the measurement around your rib cage) and your cup size (the size of your actual breasts), and always try a shirt on over the bra in question.

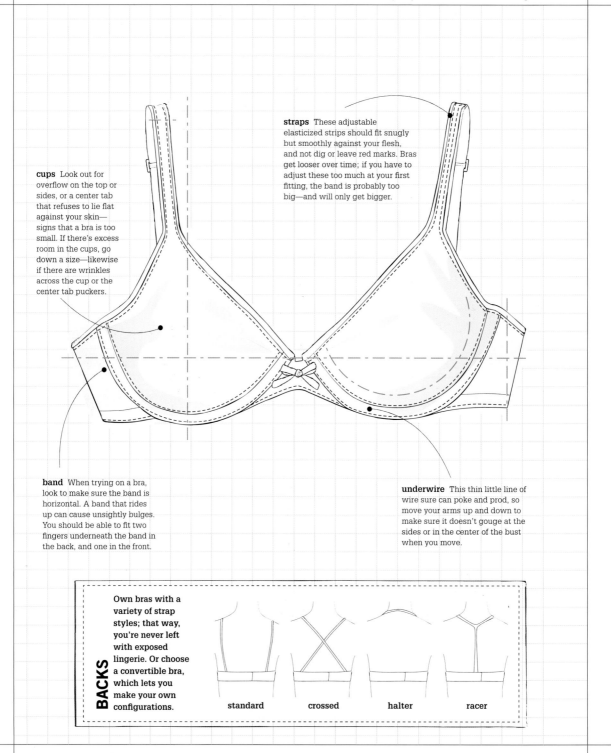

straps These adjustable elasticized strips should fit snugly but smoothly against your flesh, and not dig or leave red marks. Bras get looser over time; if you have to adjust these too much at your first fitting, the band is probably too big—and will only get bigger.

cups Look out for overflow on the top or sides, or a center tab that refuses to lie flat against your skin— signs that a bra is too small. If there's excess room in the cups, go down a size—likewise if there are wrinkles across the cup or the center tab puckers.

band When trying on a bra, look to make sure the band is horizontal. A band that rides up can cause unsightly bulges. You should be able to fit two fingers underneath the band in the back, and one in the front.

underwire This thin little line of wire sure can poke and prod, so move your arms up and down to make sure it doesn't gouge at the sides or in the center of the bust when you move.

Own bras with a variety of strap styles; that way, you're never left with exposed lingerie. Or choose a convertible bra, which lets you make your own configurations.

BACKS

standard   crossed   halter   racer

soft cup
The wide band of
this no-underwire
bra lends support
to small busts.

plunging push-up
Lifts, separates, and
pads for va-va-voom
cleavage. Perfect
for low-cut tops.

balconette
A half-cup style that
frames and boosts.
With wide straps
and fancy seams.

adhesive
A stick-on bra often
made of silicone
keeps you covered
in backless dresses.

full-coverage
Contoured cups and
no-show seams
make a smooth line
for larger busts.

demi
A thin, slight bra
that cuts straight
across the bust.
Underwire gives lift.

longline
Provides support
and smooths the
stomach for a sexy,
sleek shape.

bullet
A pointed cone
shape with circular
stitching. Naughty
yet supportive!

bandeau
A tube of stretchy
fabric. Best for small
breasts that don't
require definition.

front closure
The clasp is located
in the front for easy
quick release. No
more arm twisting!

camisole
Lace or satin
overlay conceals
cups for a delicate
mock top.

Liz Cherkasova | Late Afternoon
San Francisco, U.S.A

HOSIERY
take your pick

crew
The daily tried-and-true sock. Best in breathable cotton or warm wool.

slouchy
Thick socks with excess fabric allow for hip, oh-so-casual layers at the ankle.

back seam
Sheer hose with a sexy seam up the back. Pick a seam in a contrasting color.

fishnet
An open, diamond-shaped knit that can be small and subtle or wide and risqué.

toe
Wrap each toe in color and warmth with a goofy pair of striped toe socks.

leg warmer
Some looks call for dancewear flair—or extra warmth on your calves.

footie
A tiny sock that's nearly hidden inside a shoe. Some have fun embellishments.

ankle
A flirty sock with girlish trim that draws attention to pretty ankles.

duotone
Go mod in a pair of opaque tights with boldly contrasting leg colors.

opaque
Thin tights that are entirely solid. Try them in bright, bold colors or patterns.

pointelle
A knit stocking with an open-weave pattern. Often a chevron design.

patterned
Be darling in dots or punky in plaid and boots. Tights in fun designs abound.

ribbed
Often wool; tiny vertical grooves elongate the leg and provide texture.

sweater
Keep toasty with luxurious wool tights. Opt for tiny flecks of fun color.

footless
Opt for these when you've just got to go footloose. Perfect with flats.

thigh-high
Usually transparent with lace or satin trim. A garter belt holds them in place.

knee highs
Pay playful homage to schoolgirl days with socks that stop right at the knee.

over-the-knee
Coy and a little saucy. Try in solid cotton and pair with minis or shorts.

SWIMWEAR
take your pick

athletic
Has a higher-cut neckline and racerback for unlimited mobility.

tank
Versatile, basic, and essential. Try a low or strappy back to mix it up.

maillot
With pretty vintage details like slim straps and a sweetheart neck.

ruched
Gathers disguise imperfections to make a flattering silhouette.

pantalon
A one-piece with attached shorts is charmingly modest and play-ready.

skirted
A flirty way to feel a little more dressed when it's time to hit the beach.

strapless
Shows off the neckline. Not a lot of support for larger bustlines.

asymmetrical
The graceful single strap draws attention to the shoulders and chest.

tankini
A separate top and bottom function as one but can be mixed and matched.

monokini
A barely-attached top and bottom give the effect of a strappy bikini.

plunging
Reveals a sliver of the torso as a sophisticated way to show skin.

pretzel
A classic centerfold suit. Straps twist around the neck so the belly's bare.

sporty
A fuss-free, supportive style that's ready for beach volleyball.

bralette
A lingerie-inspired soft-cup top that's best for busts on the smaller side.

gathered
The strap gives a ruched effect on the bust. Makes a Y shape at the neck.

bandeau
A strapless top that can be a super-simple tube shape or twisted.

ruffled
Ruffles are a fun way to add shape and dimension to the bustline.

banded halter
A wide band at bottom and a strap around the neck give support.

glamour
A halter strap plus a sweetheart neckline make for a sexy take on 1950s style.

triangle
A revealing choice with string-like straps that often tie at neck and back.

knot front
A tie in front (or the look of one, if you'd rather not risk it!) takes center stage.

underwire
The supportive structure lifts, shapes, and flatters the bust.

push-up
Molded, padded cups lift and boost to create the illusion of extra curves.

ring
A ring that's usually wood or tortoise-shell draws eyes to a smaller bustline.

bikini
Revolutionized swimwear in the 1960s with its low-cut waist.

brief
The basic bottom that sits closer to the belly button than the bikini.

high waist
Pair with a glamour-girl top to get that classic pin-up look.

skirt
Choose a suit with skirted overlay as a sassy way to cover up a little.

boy short
Mini shorts let you surf or swim without fear of losing your suit.

hipster
As low as it can go, and cut straighter across the hips than other bikinis.

ruffled
A girlish bottom with bouncy ruffles that add curves to narrow hips.

side-tie
A functional tie at each hip makes it easy to strip off for skinny-dipping!

V
A deep, angled cut at the waist and superhigh-cut sides elongate legs.

string
Two teensy triangles are joined by thin strips of fabric at the sides.

brazilian
This saucy option reveals more of the lower cheeks than other bottoms.

thong
Only the daring embrace this nearly nude style that reveals the derriere.

"I was either **very, very brave** or totally crazy to have posted pictures of myself in my swimsuit online . . . but this classic **polka dot number** is too good not to share."

Carrie Harwood | Wish Wish Wish | London, U.K.

index

Carolina Engman | Fashion Squad
Stockholm, Sweden

Jessica Virgin | Vintage Virgin
Montrose, U.S.A.

Kennedy Holmes
Boston, U.S.A.

index

blogger index

Cristina Morales | La Petite Nymphéa
Barcelona, Spain

Oliwia Kijo | Variacje
Lodz, Poland

Mayo Wo | Fleas on Glam Robe
Hong Kong, China

acknowledgments

Front cover image courtesy of Shannon Sewell (Jane Aldridge). Back cover images courtesy of the credited bloggers, plus Greg Kessler (Kelly Framel), Sean Kilgore-Han (Jazzi McGill), Maurice Sampson (Liz Cherkasova), Steve Salter (Susie Lau), and Drew Tyndell (Rhiannon Leifheit).

All illustrations by Tabi Zarrinnaal.

All images of the bloggers courtesy of the credited bloggers, and all other images courtesy of Shutterstock, with the following additions:

Anik A.: 155 (Sania Claus) **Alamy:** 29 (the Supremes), 209 (Yayoi Kusama art), 215 (model in Phillip Treacy hat), 221 (Moira Shearer) **Jane and Judy Aldridge:** 1, 2–3 **Daniella Antonucci:** 44–45 (Autilia Antonucci) **Kristine Argulla:** 203 (Raez Argulla) **Montserrat Ayala:** 71 (Monica Cerino Manriquez) **Jared Balle:** 148 (Marcella Lau) **Ivar Björnsson:** 192 (Sigurbjorg Stefansdottir) **Amanda Brohman:** 134–135, 143, 167, 192 (Chantal van der Meijden) **Florian Calmel:** 103 (Lucile Vigier) **Phillip Charles Caradona:** 127 (Christina Caradona) **Kiko Lopez de Castro:** 203 (Alexandra Pereira Romero) **Tatenda Chipumha:** 138 (Camagwini) **Anthony Chow:** 9, 143 (Yuki Lo) **Marta Cieslikowska:** 143 (Coco Mayaki) **Cole Confer:** 88, 203 (Maria Confer) **Corbis:** 139 (Grace Jones), 164 (Franz Marc painting), 200 (Karl Lagerfeld), 215 (model in Rei Kawakubo design for Comme des Garçons), 221 (model in Erdem dress) **Damien Desseignet:** 78–79, 148, 192 (Aurélia Scheyé) **John Deyto:** 16–17, 19, 76–77, 104–105, 130 (Jazmine McGilbert) **Annie Fanai:** 211 (Esther Fanai) **Kristoffer Rustan Fidjestad:** 202 (Lena Fidjestad) **Martino di Filippo:** 142 (Veronica Ferraro) **Padraig Fitzgerald:** 102 (Khrystyna Marriott) **Funi:** 102 (Kanae Otomo) **Katie Gardner:** 193 (Kelli Murray) **Getty:** 109 (Anna Dello Russo), 215 (Kathleen Hanna) **Jasleen Kaur Gupta:** 71 (Sonu Bohra) **Bobby Hicks:** 27 (Keiko Groves) **Sing Ho:** 172–173 (Yuki Lo) **iStockphoto:** 29 (Tangier, stamp), 39 (boots, shorts), 90 (girls), 101 (postcard), 125 (flea market), 134 (plates), 152 (headphones) **Greg Kessler:** 50–51 (Kelly Framel) **Sean Kilgore-Han:** 76–77 (garment images) **Andreas Köttiritsch:** 71 (Eszter Farkas) **Kit Lee:** 8, 62–63, 66–67, 167 (Shini Park) **Los Angeles County Museum of Art:** 191 (Yoruba art; Digital Image © 2009 Museum Associates/LACMA/Art Resource, NY) **Rhiannon Leifheit:** 23 **Mila Mankovski:** 88 (Lida Mankovski) **Wes Mason:** 206–207 (Aimee Song) **Maria Morales:** 9, 97, 140–141, 143, 239 (Cristina Morales) **Sidney O.:** 70 (Folake Kuye Huntoon) **Michael Roy:** 31 (Jasna Zellerhoff) **Nuri Moeladi S.:** 55 (June Paski) **A. Peters:** 220–221 (Roz Jana) **JT Paradox:** 102 (Dyanna Pure) **Picture Desk:** 45 (*Picnic At Hanging Rock*, 1975 / Picnic/BEF/Australian Film Commission / The Kobal Collection), 178 (*Dynasty*, 1981-1989 / Spelling/ABC / The Kobal Collection) 178 (*Twin Peaks*, 1992 / Lynch-Frost/CIBY 2000 / The Kobal Collection), 209 (Anna Karina / The Kobal Collection) **Steve Salter:** 9, 119, 174–175 (Susie Lau) **Maurice Sampson:** 31, 55, 112–113, 229 (Liz Cherkasova) **Miguel Santana:** 126, 234–235 (Carrie Harwood) **Shannon Sewell:** 71, 178–179 (Jane Aldridge) **Luke Shadbolt:** 90–91 (Nicole Warne) **Jordy Sohier:** 143, 203 (Iris Gravemaker) **Eirik Slyngstad:** 148, 203 (Marianne Theodorsen) **Rebecca Stice:** 180–181 **Mattias Swenson:** 9, 122–123, 237 (Carolina Engman) **Michał Tokarski:** 73 (Alice Point) **Thomas Townsend:** 8 (Autilia Antonucci) **Drew Tyndell:** 8, 52–53, 100–101, 167 (Rhiannon Leifheit) **Veer:** 178 (toys) **Yannick Verhoeven:** 118 (Ilanka Verhoeven) **Ronja de Waard:** 192 (Ilanka Verhoeven) **Kasia Wabik:** 55 (Alice Point) **Bruce Weber:** 51 (Iris Apfel) **Wikimedia Commons:** 101 (*The Apartment* still), 146 (Luisa Casati), 150 (bouclé swatch), 209 (Gustav Klimt's *Portrait of Adele Bloch-Bauer,* 1907), 221 (illustration from Edmund Dulac's *The Princess and the Pea,* 1911) **Caroline Wilson:** 237 (Kennedy Holmes) **Kyle Wong:** 132–133, 239 (Mayo Wo) **Yayoi Museum:** 87 (Kasho Takabatake art) **Ariela Zaks:** 148 (Dar Mashiah) **Magda Zielasko:** 49 (Alice Point) **Jonty Van Zeller:** 8, 138–139, 205 (Funeka Ngwevela)

First published in the UK in 2011 by
Apple Press
7 Greeland Street
London NW1 0ND
www.apple-press.com

Conceived and produced by

weldonowen

415 Jackson Street, Suite 200
San Francisco, CA 94111
Telephone: 415 291 0100
Fax: 415 291 8841

www.weldonowen.com

A division of

BONNIER

Style Yourself: Inspirational Advice from the World's Hottest Fashion Bloggers

ISBN: 978-1-84543-411-3

Printed in Singapore by Tien Wah
10 9 8 7 6 5 4 3 2

Weldon Owen Inc.

CEO, President Terry Newell

VP, Sales and New Business Development Amy Kaneko

VP, Publisher Roger Shaw

Associate Creative Director Kelly Booth

Executive Editor Mariah Bear

Editor Lucie Parker

Project Editor Sabrina Yeung

Editorial Assistant Emelie Griffin

Senior Designer Stephanie Tang

Designers Michel Gadwa, Meghan Hildebrand, Delbarr Moradi, Kathryn Morgan

Production Director Chris Hemesath

Production Manager Michelle Duggan

Color Manager Teri Bell

Contributing designers:

Adrienne Aquino, Scott Erwert, Marisa Kwek, Renée Lundvall, Lisa Milestone

Special thanks to:

Mikayla Butchart, Kendra Demoura, Discount Fabrics (Irving Street, San Francisco), Jann Jones, Marianna Monacco, Katharine Moore, Caroline Thaxton, Jess Zak, and Mary Zhang.

A very special thanks to Dawn Ferguson, Kristen Strickler, and the staff of Forever 21 in Culver City, U.S.A., and the staff of Wasteland, Santa Monica, U.S.A.